Managing Groups— The Fast Track

From Good to Great

Michael Grinder

Author of *The Elusive Obvious* and
Charisma—The Art of Relationships

with Mary Yenik

Dedication

To Gail

The most important group in my world is our extended family. Gail, you are the emotional North Star of the family. Each and every member can turn to you and you are there to listen. You are fully present, you unconditionally accept us. You are our cocoon of support. Because you love me, "fame and failure are equal impostors."

Love,
Your Michael

Acknowledgments

The good Lord provided me with certain abilities; writing has come late to me in life. I sincerely thank the whole village for sharing their talents in critiquing, expanding, revising and producing this work. Special recognition goes to Rudolf Schulte-Pelkum for his diligence in helping us with the formatting and final editing of this book.

Rachel Alexander, Bob Beck, Heidi Bixby, Joyce Bovan, John Cumming, Theresa David, Colleen Dixon, Jeff Dulich, Corina Gardner, Gail Grinder, Lisa Gronseth, Hans Hommel, John Hicks, Kris Janati, Matt Jensen, Mary Mustoe, Sheila Mulchy, Carl Peck, Jerry Pavlot, Philippa Pride, Gwyn Rees, Nancy Reinman, Graeme Roberts, Ken Sayler, Sharon Sayler, Clare Smith, Robert Smith, Nancy Stout, Steve Stout, Denise Taylorson, Ashton Thomas, Mary Ann Thompson, Sue Trinder, Erik Witteborg, Jenny Witteborg, Raj Witteborg, Mary Yenik, Mike Yenik, Kendall Zoller.

With special assistance from Lorraine Adamson, Hazel-Ann Lorkins and Graham Willson.

Additional Acknowledgment

While writing this book, I lost my dear friend, Rudolf Schultz-Pelkum. Like the Tai Chi he practiced, he moved through life with grace, thoughtful intention and deliberateness. His temperament wasn't suited for conflict. He devoted himself to Zen—seeking tranquility and harmony. He supported each person's journey. He was silently proud of his family and children. He awoke each day with a readiness and ease for work and obligation. He left gentle footprints in the sands of this world. Every encounter with him included clever humor and a vulnerable sharing of each of our latest foibles. We loved each other like brothers. Death ends a life—not a relationship.

Written with deep appreciation, Michael Grinder

Editor and Contributing Author: Mary Yenik, yenik@bellsouth.net

Cover Design and Layout Assistance: Sharon Sayler, webmaster@michaelgrinder.com

Desktop Publishing: Stout Graphics, Nancy Stout, nkstout@comcast.net

ISBN: 978-1-883407-16-2

Managing Groups—The Fast Track can be purchased directly from:

Michael Grinder & Associates
16303 NE 259th Street
Battle Ground, WA 98604
(360) 687-3238; FAX (360) 687-0595
Website: http://www.michaelgrinder.com

Second Edition 2011

Table of Contents

Part Three: Dysfunctional Groups

Part Four: Healthy Groups

To be respectful of gender equality and yet provide the reader with a fluid reading style, the chapters of the book alternate the female and male pronoun usage. At the bottom of each chapter's first page, the gender pronouns for that chapter are explained.

Foreword

Fast Track is the condensed version of my *Managing Groups—the Inside Track*. *Inside Track* is the manual used in our Certification Program. *Fast Track* is the Readers Digest version of the longer work.

As a reader, you likely are drawn to Managing Groups because you want to increase your understanding of groups and how to manage them. You are either managing groups or are part of a group being managed. We know you are busy. Making time to further your professional development in group dynamics will take a commitment.

> ***You provide the time for your
> professional development, and
> we will provide the best use of your time.***

Preface

If you're involved in a service industry and have all the time in the world, you don't need this book. You can continue to bring the coffee and donuts. If you work in a results-driven industry and are fine with your level of profit and health, you don't need this book. You and others can continue to experience stress and burnout.

Fast Track is designed for those people who want to make better use of their time and make more money with less stress. From Girl Scouts to sales, from volunteering to being required to attend, from Internet meetings to boardrooms, from bowling leagues to the classroom, we are involved in and affected by group dynamics. *Fast Track* reveals in a condensed format the patterns that naturally exist in groups. The ability to interpret these patterns is useful whether you are leading a group or being led.

There are two categories of pattern recognition: "artificial" and "natural." Artificial patterns are those patterns created by people; sometimes the artificial patterns are widely known and sometimes not.

One familiar artificial pattern is the way the USA interstate highway system is coded, usually with two digits such as I-10. Highways running east-west are even numbered; those running north-south are given odd numbers. When the primary highway goes through a city, often there will be a bypass loop around the city that rejoins the highway on the other side; this auxiliary highway is given a three-digit route number (e.g., I-610) which consists of a single digit put in front of the number of the primary interstate highway (e.g., I-10). By knowing the patterns, people traveling I-10 know that I-610 bypasses a major city (in this case, Houston, Texas) and reconnects with I-10 on the other side.

Natural patterns are those that occur in nature. The famous mathematician Fibonacci discovered the patterns of spiral arrangements found in nature such as those in leaves, pinecones, and flowers. More than five centuries later, Buckminster Fuller, inventor of the geodesic dome, theorized that nothing new is invented that hasn't already occurred in nature.

There are two kinds of "pattern" geniuses. One kind of genius discovers the patterns that already exist. The second kind of genius develops practical, creative uses for the patterns. *Fast Track* attempts to do both in the arena of group dynamics.

Fast Track provides you with these patterns of group dynamics so that you can recognize what is naturally occurring in groups as easily as you can interpret the artificial patterns of interstate maps. Life is too fast for us to think our way though situations—we react instinctively. *Fast Track* educates our instincts so they will be more accurate in recognizing the patterns involved and we can better trust our instincts. Recognizing those patterns speeds up the seasoning process for someone new to an industry.

> *Recognizing those patterns speeds up the seasoning process for someone new to an industry.*

Fast Track also provides a vocabulary for those who are veterans so that they can explain their wisdom when mentoring. Having a working vocabulary of group dynamics gives you two benefits when mentoring: pattern recognition gives you and your mentee the confidence to stay calm under fire. And secondly, you both can develop the charisma of leadership with groups.

Fast Track focuses on the invisible elephant of group dynamics—effective management—especially management of the individual in a group setting.

In the past, group formation had the luxury of time. Now groups are gathered and are expected to be up and running immediately. *Fast Track* outlines the six indicators of how formed the group is and presents four techniques to increase the group's cohesiveness. The faster the group is formed, the more the person-in-charge has options—especially important when problem solving.

In the past, most successful groups had "trust" as a prerequisite. Today we need methods that have trust as a by-product. *Fast Track* provides these methods.

And for those of us who currently are or have in the past or might in the future work with dysfunctional groups, *Fast Track* provides you with a much needed confirmation of your sanity. We all are drawn to the *Serenity Prayer;* "...courage to change what I can... accept what I can't... and the wisdom to know the difference." *Fast Track* provides the blueprint "to know that difference."

FAST TRACK *is group dynamic wisdom.*

Notes

Introduction
Bird's-eye View

The Introduction provides a bird's eye view of the terrain we will be traveling. *Fast Track* is divided into four parts, each with two chapters. The following flow chart has the parts represented by the four boxes. (The chapter numbers are in parentheses.) As a reader you can read the book from beginning to end, or you can identify specific groups that hold your interest and go directly to the pertinent chapters.

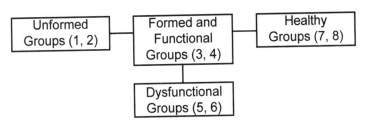

Groups can be categorized based on whether they are issue-oriented or people-oriented. These categories can be shown on two axes that form a group dynamic grid. The location of "+" and "-" has been altered from math usage. The issue-oriented axis is vertical with "high focus on issues" at the top and "low focus on issues" at the bottom. The people-oriented axis is horizontal with "high people focus" to the left and "low people focus" to the right.

To be respectful of gender equality and yet provide the reader with a fluid reading style, in this chapter the person-in-charge is referred to by male pronouns and other individuals are referred to by female pronouns.

A useful analogy is household pets. Dog-oriented groups are high people oriented. Cat-oriented groups are high issue oriented.

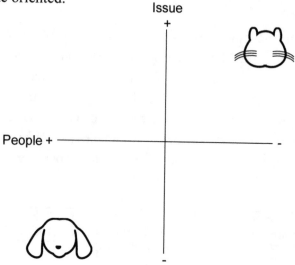

Part One: Unformed Groups

Go to Chapter One to discover the six indicators (page 16) that we use to determine whether a group is formed or unformed. Our role as the person-in-charge (page 34) is very different with an unformed vs. a formed group. By applying these six indicators to a given group, we have a clear vision of our task and options.

Go to Chapter Two to know how to accelerate the transition from unformed to formed group. And use the four techniques that accelerate the formation of a group (page 35). With a formed group we expend less energy because the group's norms are established and maintained by the group itself.

Part Two: Formed and Functional Groups

Go to Chapter Three to learn how to read the group through three key roles that members occupy, and find out how to respond to each: Outliers (page 46), Barometers (page 51), and Fostered Leaders (page 53). A leader manages the group more efficiently by forming relationships with these three key role-members.

Go to Chapter Four to learn the three methods for recognizing the culture we are interacting with. The methods give persons-in-charge subtle but dependable clues on how to succeed with a particular group. Groups are like countries; we need to know which country we are in so we can select the appropriate language to speak and know which behaviors are acceptable. Only then can we influence. Although both the cat hierarchical culture and the dog egalitarian culture can be functional, they operate very differently.

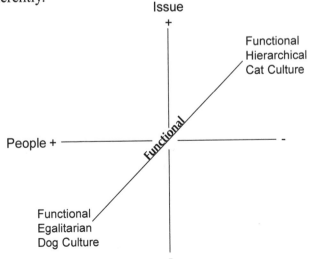

There is also a provocative presentation of how to observe.

Part Three: Dysfunctional Groups

A culture that is devoid of issue and people-orientation or is inconsistent is "dysfunctional." "Functional" and "dysfunctional" are not separate pigeonholes, but instead are gradations along a continuum.

Go to Chapter Five to learn the seven variables that influence a functional group to temporarily/occasionally become dysfunctional. If a group is dysfunctional long enough the group becomes chronically dysfunctional. The strategies that are effective with a functional group are often not transferable to a dysfunctional group. The person-in-charge's strategies for Chapters Five and Six are essential if he is to keep his own sanity as well as be effective with a dysfunctional population.

Go to Chapter Six to learn the nine variables that are so potent they can cause a group to become chronically dysfunctional. As a leader we may find ourselves inheriting a group that has been chronically dysfunctional.

Whether the group is temporarily or chronically dysfunctional, as a leader we are proactive. Either we prevent the variables from appearing or, if we can't prevent them from appearing, we are not surprised by their appearance. By recognizing the contributing variables that negatively affect group functioning, we can work to neutralize them and we can find opportunities to move the group towards becoming functional.

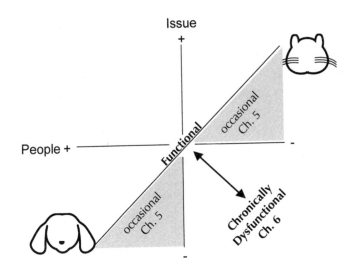

Part Four: Healthy Groups

Because Chapters Seven and Eight are the twin pinnacles of *Fast Track*, they merit a longer introduction.

A culture that blends issue-oriented with people-oriented is both functional *and* "healthy." Healthy groups are a blend of being both "High Productivity" and "High Morale." These chapters outline the traits of a healthy leader, the four universal traits of a healthy group, and the seven tools needed to be an effective negotiator.

A dog culture can be very functional, but not necessarily healthy. If someone has more time than he knows what to do with, then operating in a functional dog culture is fine. A cat culture can be very functional, but it too is not necessarily healthy. If someone craves the adrenaline rush of stress, then operating in a functional cat culture is fine.

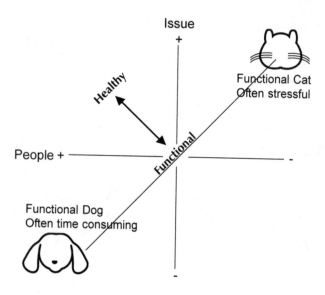

While the person-in-charge is usually more cat than the other members of the group, the role is different based on the culture of the group. The person-in-charge of a dog culture is a facilitator who seeks consensus so that harmony and morale are maintained. The person-in-charge of a cat culture is a manager who seeks to be more efficient with what the culture has always done—productivity. A healthy culture is a blend of being both issue-oriented and people-oriented. The person-in-charge is a leader. A leader questions the culture's goals and inspires members to expect more of themselves. Our goal is to be leaders.

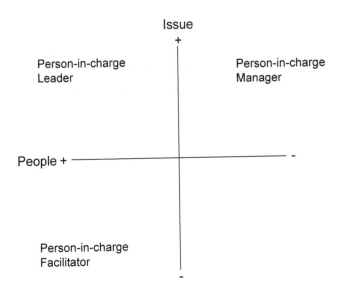

Go to Chapter Seven to compare your own traits with the traits of a healthy leader. Healthy leaders are ambitious: they want both "High Morale" and "High Productivity." They understand that they can't get high productivity without high relationships. And they know that the purpose of high relationships is to produce high results.

Chapter Seven explains how "leaders" not only have both dog and cat qualities—they know when to use them.

Also go to Chapter Seven to compare your group with a healthy group. Healthy groups share four characteristics: (1) they manage behavior (page 164); (2) they move beyond stereotyping (page 165); (3) they share leadership (page 186); and (4) when the group is irritated with an inappropriate individual, their sanity is confirmed by the person-in-charge (page 188).

Go to Chapter Eight to further your ability to negotiate with the system that your group is a part of. While *Fast Track* focuses on improving groups, we can only fully improve group dynamics by negotiating with the system that houses the group. Chapter Eight will clarify when you negotiate to increase the system's influence on your group, and when you negotiate to decrease the system's influence. There are seven perceptual tools that you can add to your negotiation toolbox.

Transition to Triangle

In addition to using the graphic of the issue-oriented and people-oriented axes, *Fast Track* uses a triangle graphic. The overlap from the axis graphic to the triangle is done by rotating the axes 45° clockwise.

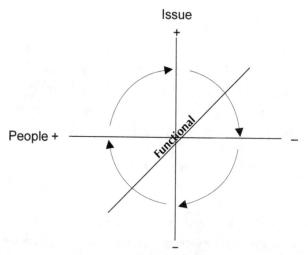

The axes are repositioned into a faded "X" pattern. The diagonal functional line is now a horizontal line.

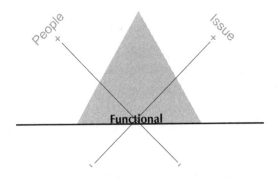

At the left end of the horizontal functional line is the dog culture with an emphasis on the individual, and at the right end is the cat culture with an emphasis on the group. This new horizontal line represents the relationship and interaction between the individuals and the group as a whole. A triangle immerges which will be *Fast Track's* icon of group dynamics.

Group dynamics is the interplay between three parties. For simplicity we will refer to these parties as P (person-in-charge), I (individual), and G (group); taken together, the three parties form a triangle.

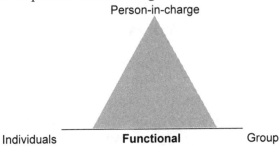

The triangle is the ideal icon for understanding group dynamics because pressure experienced by one corner equally affects the other two corners.

With this bird's-eye view, you are free to move about the group dynamics country.

How to Use This Book

To assist the reader in learning the skills in this work, the following features are included:

- **Road Map.** Each chapter opens with a road map of the territory that the chapter covers.

- **Travel Log.** Each chapter ends with a summary of the territory covered.

- **Vignettes.** Vignettes are stops at the villages. You will listen to the town folks' stories of group dynamics in that part of the country.

 - **Travel Tips.** Travel Tips are points of special interest. Often they are refinements and practical applications.

2-3
- **Free Worksheets.** There are free downloadable worksheets for all the book's major concepts at www.michaelgrinder.com. The first number indicates the chapter followed by the worksheet number. For example, 2-3 indicates Chapter Two, third worksheet.

- **Text and Graphics.** When you travel, you often download a map from the Internet. Usually the printout has two different forms of the same information. Your left-brain focuses on the step-by-step understanding of the journey you are about to take. Your right-brain receives a picture, a schematic. *Fast Track* satisfies your two different learning styles. The text appeals to your left brain. The text is designed to build from one specific concept to the next specific concept. And the graphics appeal to some readers' right brain.

Chapter One
Unformed Groups

Road Map

When people gather for the first time, they are really not a group—as represented by the dashes that make up the letter "G." The person-in-charge's goal is to move an unformed group into being a formed group. Her role is different when the group is unformed than formed. She has to be able to identify if the group is formed or not formed to effectively select the appropriate role. This chapter provides the six indicators which reveal how unformed or formed the group is:

1. **Where is the group looking?**
2. **What is the speed of the transition into an activity?**
3. **What is the speed of transition from an activity back to the person-in-charge?**
4. **How well do the members know each other?**
5. **Who is providing the safety?**
6. **Is there a unisance of response?**

Management Challenges

Managing an unformed group consumes more of the person-in-charge's energy as she is the source for productivity, morale, and safety. A formed group provides its own productivity, morale, and safety.

To be respectful of gender equality and yet provide the reader with a fluid reading style, in this chapter the person-in-charge is referred to by female pronouns and other individuals are referred to by male pronouns.

There are two management situations that are particularly challenging. The first is when the person-in-charge is managing an individual and is concerned about how the group might be interpreting it. The second is when the person-in-charge is managing the group and is concerned about how an individual might be interpreting it.

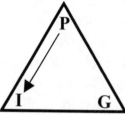 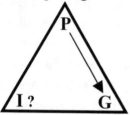

To understand how the person-in-charge can effectively handle these two management situations, she must first determine if the group is formed or unformed. When a group is unformed, the person-in-charge's choices are limited. On the other hand, when a group is formed, the person-in-charge has more options. For a sneak look at one of the options, see Indicator No. 5 (page 23).

Six Indicators of Group Formation

There are six indicators that chart a group's progress from unformed to formed. Keep in mind that different cultures will have slight variations on how they display the indicators. For the purposes of illustration, Mediterranean people tend to be more gregarious than the more reserved people from northern Germany.

1-1

1. Where is the group looking?

Unformed: On the first day of the gathering, the participants are waiting for the start of the meeting. Since they don't know each other, they are likely to be looking at the front of the room or down at written materials, thereby indicating their dependence on the person-in-charge.

Formed: Eventually the participants get to know each other. At subsequent gatherings the members are talking and looking at each other while waiting for the start of the meeting.

> ### Vignette: Call to Order
>
> Ashley is about to open the first meeting of the regional managers. The people are awkwardly silent and stiff.
>
> Ashley always tries to start the meeting on time. For the members who value punctuality, starting the first meeting promptly sets a tone that she is reliable and dependable. She knows that she needs to provide clear expectations such as the need for punctuality. As the members become familiar with one another, they will be comfortable with subsequent meetings starting "almost" on time.

Summary: At the start of a meeting, where members look is an indicator of how formed the group is. If the members are silent and looking at the front of the room or looking down, the group is unformed. If the members are looking at each other and talking, the group is formed. As an observer, watch where the members are looking or listen for the degree of silence vs. chit-chat.

2. What is the speed of the transition into an activity?

1-1 *

The second indicator of how formed a group is, is the length of time it takes members to begin a cooperative

---

*The same worksheet is used several times.

activity. Because trainings are gatherings where it is likely the attendees don't know each other, trainings are an ideal environment to study group formation. Trainings with lots of interactions reveal these six indicators most clearly.

Unformed: When a trainer announces a cooperative activity, how fast do the participants switch from being focused on the person-in-charge to looking and interacting with their peers? When the group is not yet formed, the participants often will start to turn their heads toward their partners, but their eyes are still looking at the person-in-charge. The participants have come to the gathering because of the person-in-charge, not the other members.

Formed: Over time, the participants become familiar with their mates. When a cooperative activity is announced, the members readily turn both their heads and eyes to their partners.

Vignette: "Turn to your colleague..."

There are 24 communication behavioral skills that Olga teaches in her three-day program. When she first asks the participants to turn to their neighbor and practice the first skill, they are slow to engage with each other. Because of their hesitation, she provides a specific script so they can be successful.

By the end of the second day, the members are so familiar with role-play and so comfortable with each other that sometimes Olga isn't finished explaining the instructions before they begin the exercise.

Summary: When members are slow to engage with each other, then the group is more unformed than formed. If the members are quick to engage with each other, then the group is formed.

Travel Tips—Visual Information

When we are in charge of an unformed group, the members need us to be competent in setting the outcomes and indicating how we are going to get there. When we visually post an agenda and instructions for cooperative activities, we are seen as competent and they feel safe. When members are safe, they form as a group quicker.

3. What is the speed of transition from an activity back to the person-in-charge?

1-1

The third indicator is the speed with which members disengage from each other and refocus on the person-in-charge.

Unformed: The rate of speed from a cooperative activity back to the person-in-charge indicates how bonded a group is. When the person-in-charge requests attention from members engaged in a cooperative activity, the participants quickly turn their heads toward the person-in-charge; the group isn't formed yet. This indicates that the person-in-charge is still more important to the participants than the members are to one other.

Formed: Over time the participants form bonds with one other. When the person-in-charge indicates a transition back to the person-in-charge, the participants have the urge to finish their last sentence or, in some cases, paragraph before returning to the person-in-charge's instruction. In a formed group there is as much learning and productivity produced from members as there is from the person-in-charge.

Vignette: "Hey, I am over here!"

On the first day when Olga calls the group back from a skill development activity, they come back very quickly By the third day, the group is fully formed and people not only quickly engage in exercises, they are also reluctant to disengage.

Olga was concerned that she could lead a group for one day or a day and half but felt her command was slipping after that. Olga shared her concerns with a veteran colleague, Guy. Guy explained that the state of group formation changes over time. In a shorter program, dependence on the presenter is natural and beneficial. With longer programs, the goal is to transfer the dependence on the trainer to interdependence among the participants. And, at the same time, the trainer has to know how to interpret the shift in dependence.

Summary: The speed with which a group stops their cooperative activities and turns their attention back to the presenter indicates how formed the group is. When people don't know each other well, they are quick to disengage from an activity and refocus on the person-in-charge. If the group is formed, they are slow to disengage with their neighbors and refocus on the person-in-charge.

 Travel Tips—Getting Attention

As the group becomes formed, they are slower to respond when we ask for attention As this happens, it is natural for us to think we are losing control. A wiser view is to simply understand that they are more formed—more bonded together—than they used to be. To fully enjoy the benefits of a formed group we must use two precise management skills: *Freeze Body*[1] and *ABOVE (Pause) Whisper*.[2]

Freeze Body

When the person-in-charge is still when asking the group for attention, her stillness non-verbally signals the members to be still also, to simply stop what they are doing.

ABOVE (Pause) Whisper

When the group is large or noisy, we can reinforce our message of "Please give me your attention" with a voice pattern that has three parts. A full sentence might go unnoticed as our words become part of the background cacophony. Instead, say 1 to 4 words ABOVE the group's collective voice volume. When we use this loud (ABOVE) voice pattern, the group might perceive us as being in a bad mood. To minimize this possibility, we do the ABOVE a few steps from where we are actually going to speak. Once the group is sufficiently quiet, we do the second part: we simultaneously look down, drop our frozen hand gesture and walk a few steps towards where we will speak.[3] Lastly, when we are in the new location we look up and say a phrase or two in a friendly Whisper. Then we resume our regular voice pattern.

1-1

4. How well do the members know one another?

Unformed: At the beginning of a gathering, participants often don't know each other. No one knows who are the smarter participants, the troublemakers, the questioners or clowns. In an unformed group, how ever the person-in-charge treats each person is how the rest of the group believes they will be treated. At first, then, the person-in-charge is gentle with each member, even the inappropriate ones.

Formed: In time, the group members increase their familiarity with each other. The participants come to know who is likely to act in certain ways. Those who are inappropriate are seen as different from the rest of the group. How the person-in-charge treats these members doesn't reflect on how the person-in-charge will treat anyone else.

Vignette: Ice-breakers

Samantha, the keynote presenter, opened with, "Sometimes a presenter will ask an unformed group engage in ice-breaking activities in order to accelerate the speed with which members get to know each other. However, icebreakers don't always work well, and here's why.

"Dog-oriented people are more gregarious than cat-oriented people. The dogs welcome such socializing interactions. Cats can openly resent them as evidenced by an active or passive refusal to participate. If we are uncertain as to whether the individuals will go along with the ice-breaker, it is safer to use mingling activities under the banner of relevant information, as in, 'This convention is four days long. You will have free time to interact with people from the many regions in which our company does business. Take this opportunity to get to know each other so that you can use your free time wisely. Put on your card: your name, region, department you are in, how many years you have been with the company and two burning questions that you would like to dialogue about.'"

5. Who is providing the safety?

1-1

Unformed: At the beginning of the group formation, the atmosphere is influenced more by the person-in-charge than by any other single variable. For the sake of the group, the person-in-charge needs to appear confident and intelligent.[4] Any difficulties that arise need to be resolved by the person-in-charge. This includes difficulties involving the environment (temperature, working areas), schedule, expectations, and people.

Formed: As the members become a group, they provide their own emotional, physical, and intellectual safety. For example, if the room temperature is not right, members will initiate changing the thermostat. If the coffee isn't right someone will look into it. If someone is confused, members will step in to help. If there is an unexpected disruption in the schedule, the group feels empowered to grapple with it.

The next vignette shows the importance of a group being formed especially when handling a crisis. This vignette is about the actual events of July 7, 2005, the terrorist bombing of the London subways. Because of the vividness of this very real experience, you decide whether to read it or skip to the summary on page 25.

Vignette: July 7, 2005

I was conducting an on-going London training during the summer of 2005. I had met with this group for four days in May. On July 7, I was greeting the participants on our first day of the second module. Shortly after 9:00 a.m., people came in saying that some members might be late because of delays on the tube system. Within 30 minutes, "delays" turned into "rumors" about explosions on one or more trains. We were reduced back to basic needs.

I immediately moved the two flipcharts from the stage and placed them on the side wall. I asked two participants who had emerged as leaders during the previous module to help the group brainstorm what were our needs and resources. With the phone lines jammed, we cautioned each other to stay calm and resist speculating. By the end of day, the sharing of food and comfort was overwhelming.

Of course, we later learned that these four suicide explosions constituted the largest and most deadly terrorist attack on London in its history: 56 people killed, 700 injured and the transport and mobile telecommunications infrastructure crippled severely on the first day.

Commentary: If the bombings had occurred during the first day of the May training, I would have had to direct how we handled the crisis. Simply, unconsciously the group would have expected me to solve....

Luckily, the group was formed from the first module. I will always be thankful for Helen and Joan for handling the flipcharts; and for John, Angie and others for caring for those in shock. Handling the crisis from the sidewall decontaminated our stage area. We were able to continue our learning during that module.

Summary: In general, people need safety to participate and learn. When the group is unformed, the safety is provided by the person-in-charge. As the group becomes formed, the group provides its own safety.

When dogs know each other, they feel safe and participate more. Dogs remind us of Aesop's fable about the lion and the mouse: *"No* act of *kindness, no matter how small,* is ever wasted." Cats provide their own safety and individually decide about their level of participation. Cats are self-selective: they ask, "What's in it for me?" Once they know what they want, they value effectiveness and efficiency—"Acts of efficiency, however small, are always appreciated."

6. Is there a unisance of response?

1-1

Unformed: In an unformed group, members tend to respond to the person-in-charge in a staggered manner. Some are ready to enter into cooperative activity and others are not. Some will like the person-in-charge's humor and others won't like it. If they are asked to turn to page 25 of the report, participants begin to open their books at different times, frequently in waves. When the group comes back from lunch, how many waves are there? The less a group is formed as a unit, the more likely it is that there is a lack of unisance of response.

Formed: The unisance of response is the single clearest indicator that a group is formed. This includes laughing, moving into small group activities, quieting, coming back from breaks on time. From a group dynamic standpoint, it is more important that the group does what they do in unison than that some of them do what the person-in-charge desires. For example, if the whole group comes back from lunch ten minutes late, that is more important than if half of the people come back on time and the other half ten minutes late.[5]

Vignette: Humorous Harriet Meets Slim

Harriet opened her programs with jokes that usually had the audience laughing and bonding together. At other times, however, half of the audience loved her humor and the other half didn't. She wanted to understand why her humor produced varied reactions. She asked around, "Who is the best consultant?" After hearing that "Slim" was "the best," she phoned and made an appointment for Slim to drop by.

When the 70 year-old Slim, boots and all, walked into Harriet's office, Harriet's jaw dropped. Slim, a master reader of humans, immediately opened with reassurance, "Remember they will be hiring you—not me. I am here to help you."

He popped open his laptop, "Let's look at this first opening you sent me. They love your lines and obviously, you and the audience are bonding by having fun. Now study this second opening: some people are laughing and some are not.

"In both cases your humor is fine. Don't focus on improving your humorous openings; instead, focus on the group dynamics. Let's look at the second opening again. The humor isn't working, but you continue. You are splitting your group into a subgroup who likes your humor and one that doesn't.

"Remember, your goal is a unified group. When humor works, it is the fastest way to get people relaxed and bonded. But some groups don't want you to be funny—they want to work. If humor isn't working, it's okay to stop trying to be funny. With these groups, first get them working, then go back to your humor."

Summary: When people do things together, at the same time, it is an indication that the group is cohesive. "Unisance" is both evidence of a bonded group and a method for bonding the group (page 35). The most sophisticated evidence of a bonded group is when they breathe together. Humor is the most acceptable method of getting people to bond; literally, we start to laugh (i.e., exhale) at the same time and then we stop laughing (i.e., inhale) at the same time. Another method for quickly bonding a group is singing, especially before special meetings and events such as sport events.

Travel Log

The next two boxes summarize the terrain we have traveled in Chapter One.

> Three questions dominate group dynamics:
>
> - *Where is the group looking?*
> - *Is there a unisance of response?*
> - *How are they breathing?**

---

*The third question comes from pages 64 and 85.

Indicators of Group Formation

Unformed

Formed

1. Where is the group looking?

At person-in-charge

At each other

2. How fast do the individuals make the transition from the person-in-charge into a group activity?

Initially they turn heads towards each other while still looking at person-in-charge.

They turn eyes and heads towards each other.

3. How fast do the individuals make the transition from a group activity back to being attentive to the person-in-charge?

Very quick

Slower

4. How well do the members know one another?

5. Who is providing the safety?

Person-in-charge provides

Group provides

6. How is the unisance of response? (This is the most important indicator.)

Chapter Two
Transition to a Formed Group

Road Map

This chapter gives step-by-step accelerated methods to change an unwieldy, unformed group into a well-functioning, formed group. This chapter focuses on two major concepts:

The Changing Role of the Person-in-charge—It explores how the person-in-charge facilitates the formation and adjusts his style to be in sync with the group as they become more formed. The second major concept is the four techniques that accelerate the formation of a group:

Echo—get the group to do activities together

Acknowledge—guide the group through difficulties

Silence—use silence to blend a group

Your Hands—use hand gestures to meld a group

To fully appreciate the benefits of a formed group the following overview is offered.

As mentioned in the Introduction, most groups end up being either issue-oriented or people-oriented. These categories can be shown on two axes that form a group dynamic grid. The issue-oriented axis is vertical, with "high focus on issues" at the top and "low focus on issues" at

---

To be respectful of gender equality and yet provide the reader with a fluid reading style, in this chapter the person-in-charge is referred to by male pronouns and other individuals are referred to by female pronouns.

the bottom. The people-oriented axis is horizontal, with "high people focus" to the left and "low people focus" to the right.

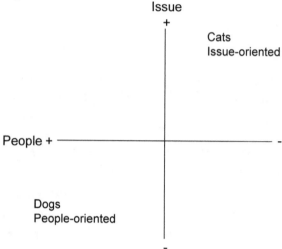

A new gathering of people is just that—"a gathering." The gathering is not a group; we cannot place a gathering on the grid because we don't yet know what type of group it will be, that is, whether their focus will be on *people* or on *issues*. As the people form a group, they usually end up either in the bottom left quadrant of "high people-oriented / low issue-oriented" or the top right quadrant of "high issue-oriented / low people-oriented."

Predicting

Paying attention to just two variables, a person-in-charge will be able to predict early which quadrant the group will end up in. His ability to predict helps him determine the appropriate role to play and what leadership style will be most effective. The variables are 1) the purpose of the group and 2) the composition of the members. Knowing whether a group is going to be more people-oriented or issue-oriented will also let the person-in-charge know his range of options. An easy way of understanding which "oriented" quadrant a group will gravitate towards is to use the analogy of household pets—dogs and cats.

Dogs

Dogs come when you call them. Dogs are people oriented—they want to please others. Their motivations, expectations, and outcomes come from interdependence with others. Typically, people-oriented groups are found in industries that are service-focused and have less clear performance criteria. This includes education, charities, and social work. Dogs are attracted to "giving-to-others." Dogs like to operate from their "person." Because of these traits, dog cultures tend to be egalitarian. People who work long enough and successfully enough in a humanitarian industry tend to increase their dogness.

A person's voice pattern indicates if the individual is dog-like and suited for the line of work they are in. Dogs are more likely to use an approachable voice pattern. They move their heads while speaking, causing their voice to be rhythmic ($\wedge\wedge$). Then at the end of phrases and sentences, they move their head up resulting in an intonation of a curl up, almost like a question. ($\wedge\wedge\uparrow$). This is the voice of the flight attendant.

Cats

When you call cats, they have an answering machine and will get back to you later. Cats tend to focus on what they want—their issues. Typically, issue-oriented groups are found in profit-driven industries that have clear performance criteria so that results can be measured. Cats are attracted to competition. Their motivations, expectations, and outcomes come from inside them.* Cats like to operate from "position." Cat cultures tend to be hierarchical. People who work long enough and successfully enough in a profit-driven industry tend to increase their catness.

A person's voice pattern indicates whether the individual is more suited for people-oriented cultures or issue-oriented cultures. Cats are likely to use a credible voice pattern, a reliable indicator that they would be well-suited for an issue-oriented environment. They hold their heads still while speaking, causing their voices to be flat (————). Then at the end of phrases and sentences, they move their head down resulting in an intonation of a curl down (————). This is the voice of the airplane pilot.

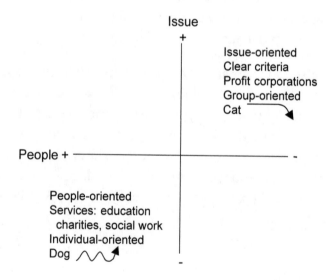

Issue
+

Issue-oriented
Clear criteria
Profit corporations
Group-oriented
Cat

People + ———————————————— -

People-oriented
Services: education
  charities, social work
Individual-oriented
Dog

-

----

*For more information, we recommend a companion book, *Charisma—the Art of Relationships*. *Charisma* focuses on one-on-one communication, while *Fast Track* focuses on group dynamics. In that sense, *Fast Track* is the "group dynamics" application of *Charisma*."

To categorize people as dogs or cats would be incomplete without three cautions:

1. Continuum, not pigeonholes. *Fast Track* sees dogs and cats as behavioral profiles, not personality profiles like Myers-Briggs or DISC.*

2. Depends on our own expectations. We are more dog or cat compared to someone else—it is relative.

3. Depends on the situation. The third caution is that we have both a dog persona and a cat persona inside of ourselves. Our display of "cat and dog" depends on the situation.

The following statement summarizes these cautions: "In the context of_____, compared to _____, I am more (cat or dog)."[6]　(individual or group)

Functional

Both a dog service-oriented culture and a cat profit-oriented culture can be equally functional. But they look very different. A dog in a functional cat culture perceives the group as dysfunctional because they lack manners and tact, they are insensitive to the individual, and they don't take time to care. A cat in a functional dog culture perceives the group as dysfunctional because they lack efficiency and effectiveness, they are slow to make decisions, and they don't take time to check the bottom line.

———

*DISC is an inventory system whereby people understand themselves and others in a non-judgment manner. It is based on a group of psychological inventories developed by John Geier and based on the 1928 work of psychologist William Moulton Marston.

2-1

The Person-in-charge's Changing Role

Most groups have an individual whose title is "person-in-charge." This individual is usually more cat than the other members of the group. The role or function of the person-in-charge is based on the culture of a given group. Because a dog culture is people-oriented, the doglike group tends to avoid conflict. The person-in-charge of the dog group is a facilitator who seeks consensus so that harmony and morale are maintained. Because a cat culture is issue-oriented, the catlike group tends to be goal oriented. The person-in-charge of the cat group is a manager who seeks to be more efficient with what the culture has always done—productivity.

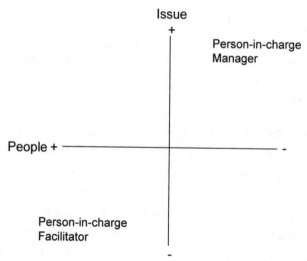

Pilot vs. Flight Attendant

The difference between how the person-in-charge operates *initially* compared to how the person-in-charge will *eventually* manage is analogous to airline personnel. The person-in-charge is the pilot and the group members are the passengers. Passengers expect the pilot to speak in a credible voice; this pattern[7] reassures passengers that they are in good hands. The flight attendants, on the other hand, are expected to speak in an approachable voice; this pattern[8] conveys friendliness as attendants seek input from the passengers: "Would you like a beverage?"

Blending a Group is EASY

The person-in-charge's goal with an unformed group is to quickly form the group by using four techniques.[9] The techniques' initials spell out the acronym EASY.

EASY—Echo

2-2

Unisance (page 25) isn't just an indicator of how formed a group is; it is also a method for accelerating group formation. "Echo" is a technique that artificially increases unisance in a group.

Different cultures allow different styles of unisance. Only do techniques that are acceptable to the culture. Here are two sample techniques for speeding up unisance of response: oral and physical.

Oral Echo

The person-in-charge can orally structure the members' response so that unisance occurs. He says a new word or sentence and has the group repeat it in unisance. The presenter can drag his voice out as he says, "Let's say it together: r e a d y." This is especially helpful when the presenter uses hand gestures that remind one of an orchestra leader.

Physical Echo

The military uses marching as physical unisance. Anyone who has been in the service or witnessed cadets marching knows that the purpose isn't just physical conditioning—it is to bond the unit together. Physical activities that bond participants include singing, dancing, and laughing. For a number of years, my brother Thomas and I co-presented. To get in sync with each other, we would juggle together before we started.

E**A**SY—Acknowledge

2-3

An unformed group becomes formed faster when members perceive the person-in-charge as competent. Oftentimes, being competent is simply a matter of the person-in-charge acknowledging what is occurring. Sometimes it is simply indicating that he knows the composition of the group. Examples include:

- "How many of you have traveled far enough so you are not sleeping at home tonight?" or "How many are attending from company 'x'? … from 'y' company ?"

Being Proactive with Volatility

The most critical situation for a person-in-charge to acknowledge is when something volatile is about to happen. Remember the last time you were on an airplane taxiing down the runway and, as the plane climbed, you experienced considerable turbulence. If the pilot had come on, "This is your captain speaking. We may be experiencing some turbulence…" you might have thought, "Right, Sherlock! Who is the bozo flying this plane?" We distrust people in positions of authority who tell us after-the-fact what we already know. This is a reactive acknowledgment. Competence is when the person-in-charge indicates *before* we experience "x" that we will be experiencing "x."

A pint of proactive acknowledgment is worth a gallon of reactive acknowledgment.[10] Let's replay the same scene with a proactive acknowledgment. You are on the tarmac, and the pilot says, "This is your captain speaking. We are third for take off. As you can see outside, there are some fronts passing through our area. We have been safely taking off and landing all day. There will be some turbulence as we climb. Make sure your seat belt is fastened—we will be fine." Then when we experience the turbulence we feel much more secure because the person-in-charge knew ahead of time what was about to happen and informed us.

Sometimes, a person-in-charge is presenting to a tough group. Instead of ignoring what is going on, the person-in-charge can simply acknowledge the group's resistance. For example, "Some of you/us may not like to do role-play." Once the person-in-charge has done the surface acknowledgment, he can add information. This additional information often lessens the resistance: "Some of you/us may not like to do role-plays, and yet research shows that by doing the role-plays, people are better able to duplicate their new skills in the real world."

2-4

A more sophisticated method for acknowledging is to address not only what the people are resisting but why they are resisting. By addressing their motivation for resisting, the person-in-charge has more options. The easiest way of getting to the intention level is to follow up the surface acknowledgment (for example, "You may not like to do role-plays") with this sentence, "And there is a good reason why." Then say the reason.

Vignette: "Why should you be here?"

As Shawn walked to the front of the 50 telemarketers, he could both see and feel their cold stares. He began with "Morning." He paused long enough to indicate that he could breathe deeply and stay relaxed even in such a hostile environment. He then walked two steps to the flipchart and read, "Phone Skills. 9-noon."

He paused again. Then he looked down and simultaneously turned and started to walk to the other side of the front. As he passed the center point, he was still looking down when he softly said, "Before we begin..." Arriving at the far side, he faced the bewildered audience, "If I were you [long pause] I wouldn't want to be here. Some of you might even be tempted to not take any notes. [Another long pause.] You have too much work to do back at your desk." [He gestured and looked at the outside wall in the direction of their work stations.] [He paused again.] He turned back to the presentation flipchart.

Shawn had first acknowledged their resistance, "...wouldn't want to be here." He even talked about the inappropriate behavior of "...tempted not to take any notes." Even cats appreciate it when a person-in-charge can calmly talk about the "invisible elephants."

Shawn then switched from a surface focus about inappropriate behavior such as "not taking notes" to the motivation behind the surface "too much work to do...." By switching to the motivation level he can honestly agree with them. The reasons why people do things, even negative things, stem from positive purposes.

The process of acknowledging people's surface resistance and then progressing to acknowledging the motivation behind the surface resistance increases the audience's receptivity to the reframe. In the previous vignette Shawn could offer this reframe:

> **Vignette: "Why should you be here?"**
> (continued)
>
> Half way back to the presentation flipchart, Shawn turns and whispers, "How long would you wait to see if today's skills might actually save you time and energy?"

One way to increase the likelihood that the group will let the person-in-charge offer the reframe is to change his language from "You don't want to be here," to *"Part* of you may not want to be here."

Here is Shawn opening with several levels of acknowledgment:

> **Vignette: "Why should you be here?"**
> (revised)
>
> Shawn opens with "Morning." He pauses long enough to indicate that he can breathe deeply and stay relaxed even in such a hostile environment. He then walks two steps to the flipchart and reads, "Phone Skills. 9-noon."
>
> He pauses again. Then he looks down and simultaneously turns and starts to walk to the other side of the front. As he passes the center point, he is still looking down as he softly says, "Before we begin..." Arriving at the far side, he faces the bewildered audience, "If I were you [long pause]

I wouldn't want to be here. Part of you might even be tempted not to take any notes. [Another long pause.] You have too much work to do back at your desk." [He gestures and looks at the outside wall in the direction of their work stations.] [He pauses again.]

Half way back to the presentation flipchart, Shawn turns and whispers, "There may be another part of you that is thinking, 'How long would I give any speaker to see if what we are going to do will actually save me time and energy?"

Shawn uses different locations. By mentioning the negative content at the acknowledgment location off to the side, Shawn preserves the presentation location. When he moves away from the acknowledgement location, the group is likely to have amnesia about the negative items he had mentioned "over there;" as a result, they can concentrate better on the rest of the agenda items.

2-5

EA<u>S</u>Y—Silence

EASY's third method of bonding a group together is silence. To understand how silence impacts people, think of a time when you were meeting someone for the first time. Maybe you were on a date or meeting another couple for dinner. In an unformed group, silence is dreaded. However, in a formed group silence is comfortable, and even valued. Silence is one of the ways that I know my wife, Gail, is my best friend. We can be next to each other and talk or be silent.

Vignette: Encounter Groups

As a student at Loyola, I represented the university at a humanistic weekend. As we students from the Los Angeles area listened to the opening remarks about the need for better communication, we were challenged to increase our realness, and to become more authentic and genuine humans.

We were divided into groups of 8 to 12 and assigned to certain rooms. When we entered the rooms, more than one of us were taken aback by the lack of chairs—all we saw were pillows forming a circle.

No one was identified as the person-in-charge. There was silence. When someone did finally talk, the awkward silence that followed was associated with that person. I found a spot on the floor to focus on, I was afraid to look up and risk making eye contact with someone else. I felt so lost and unsafe I almost bolted a few times during the first five hours (which was actually thirty minutes).

By the end of the second day, we were formed; when someone did speak, everyone listened attentively. When there was silence, the group was unmistakably comfortable. The silence was a welcome opportunity to be reflective.

The person-in-charge of an unformed group assists their progress in becoming formed by intentionally opening his presentation with frequent pauses, moments of silence that are longer than normal. These mini-silences are a major contributor to others feeling accepted. During the silence, the lower and more comfortably he breathes, the more people feel accepted. The sooner people feel accepted, the faster they bond together.

2-6

EAS<u>Y</u>—Your Hands

Acknowledge was EASY's second technique for bonding a group together; "Your Hands" is the non-verbal level of Acknowledge. When the person-in-charge is acknowledging any diversity at a gathering, then the technique of "Your Hands" can be used. For example, "Some of us [person-in-charge extends his left hand towards the sub-group in the room] are from Marketing. And some of us [person-in-charge extends his right hand] are here from Human Resources." With each hand representing the different parts of the group, the presenter can now say, "We are here at this retreat to outline [as the word "outline" is mentioned the person-in-charge claps both hands together and moves them to the flipchart] next year's..."

Travel Log

The person-in-charge forms the group as fast as possible. The benefits of a formed group are many:

- The person-in-charge can manage with influence instead of power.

- The group owns whatever problems arise.

- When a disagreement arises among members, the parties assign positive intentions to those they disagree with.

- If the person-in-charge knows the culture of the group, he can trust his perception and instincts.

- The person-in-charge can readily recognize the appropriate role for himself to play.

- It takes less energy to be a person-in-charge of a formed group. The members rely on one other. The person-in-charge has more energy at the end of the day.

Three Cautions

To categorize people as dogs or cats would be to miss the point of *Fast Track*. Three cautions were given to temper any over-generalizations. The following statement summarizes these cautions: The following statement summarizes these cautions: "In the context of_____, compared to _____, I am more (cat or dog)."
                                   (individual or group)

EASY

Four techniques accelerate an unformed group into becoming a formed group.

E—Echo: any activity that has everyone doing something at the same time.

A—Acknowledge: A group, especially an unformed group, feels safe when the person-in-charge is competent. For example, he acknowledges that he knows what is going to happen before it happens. Or he acknowledges that he knows the composition of the group.

S—Silence: the person-in-charge is comfortable with silence. And since "comfortable silence" suggests a high level of familiarity, it subliminally conveys that the group is already formed.

Y—Your Hands: when the person-in-charge is doing verbal acknowledgment, he can represent the diverse groups via "your hands." By bringing his hands together, he symbolically blends the groups together.

Chapter Three
Functional Groups

To understand group dynamics, the person-in-charge suspends her perception and is attentive to how the group sees the situation.

Road Map

Group dynamics and individuals influence each other. The group can be partially understood by studying the individuals who will make up a group and the individual can only be understood in the context of the group. Only certain individuals need to be understood to read the group. This chapter looks at the individuals who fulfill the roles of outliers, barometers, and fostered leaders. The chapter also looks at the "Identity Size" of all members.

1. Outliers

Outliers are members who don't fit the group's norms. The group notices the outliers more than the other members. Therefore, the group notices when the person-in-charge interacts with outliers. The person-in-charge's reputation is often based on how she handles the outliers.

2. Barometers

Barometers are members of a subgroup who react earlier than other members. The person-in-charge notices these

---

To be respectful of gender equality and yet provide the reader with a fluid reading style, in this chapter the person-in-charge is referred to by female pronouns and other individuals are referred to by male pronouns.

early responders to determine if she is getting the response she wants. If not, she adjusts what she is doing.

3. Fostered Leaders

Fostered Leaders are members who represent a value that is missing in the group culture. The person-in-charge fosters these members so that the missing value becomes part of the culture.

4. Group Members' Identity Size

Group Members' Identity Size describes how much the members identify with each other at any given time. The person-in-charge adjusts her style based on whether the members are identifying with each other or not.

Reading a Group

3-1

1. Outliers

The term "outliers" describes the people who are outside the group's norms, people who are different; the group notices them. Because the group is watching, the person-in-charge's reputation is often based on how she manages the outliers.

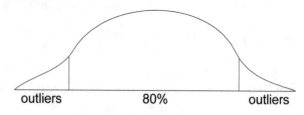

outliers   80%   outliers

Here are the four evolutionary stages of group development. At each stage, the norms change and who the outliers are will change also.

1. Group is unformed. Unique physical appearance is noticed. Group notices tall or short, old or young, anything unusual.

2. Group is starting to form. Unique behaviors are noticed. Group notices things such as punctuality, walking gait, talking speed, amount of note taking, how people enter a room, how they sit.

3. Group is formed and functioning. Unique style is noticed. Group notices things such as intelligence, skepticism, competency, confidence, humor, and curiosity. They notice thinking styles, such as visual or auditory, big versus small picture, concrete versus abstract, and random versus sequential.

4. Group is healthy. Values are noticed. Group notices values, beliefs, presuppositions, and attitudes. If there is a crisis, one's character is noticed.

Chapter Three focuses on the outliers of a formed and functioning group.* Based on the group's norms, those outliers who exceed the group's positive norms are seen as positive leaders. Those outliers who are deficit in the group's norms are seen as negative leaders.

A legend is someone who is known by people as an outlier in some unusually positive way. Just the mention of the legend's name carries attention.

Positive Leader's Voice and Timing

The better a person's timing, the more likely it is that the individual will become a leader. There are many variables

*Chapter Seven will delve into stereotyping (See page 165).

that affect a person's timing: eye contact, voice speed, voice volume, breathing, and gestures. Although each of these variables can enhance good timing when used properly, the single most powerful key to good timing is the pause.

> *The pause is the single most essential non-verbal aspect of effective timing.*

Vignette: Let me try that again

Angelina sat and pouted. She had just offered a valid suggestion that was not even given the time of day.

Resisting the temptation to feel sorry for herself, she looked down at her laminated bookmarker from the course she had taken in non-verbal communication. She reviewed what she had done. She realized that she had not paused long enough; the group may have thought, "Well, if she isn't confident about her idea, why should we give it attention?"

She waited for an appropriate opening and shot up her hand. As the chair recognized her, she spoke in a strong voice, reinforced by a frozen hand gesture, "I was thinking..." She stopped mid-sentence. Her pause seemed like forever to her. But she peripherally watched the members to see when they finally stopped holding their breath. That is when she quietly went into her spiel. She was pleased that she remembered to pause after each key point and freeze her hand during the silence to indicate that she wasn't finished yet.

On the subway ride home that night, she smiled— yes, they were going to look into her idea.

Outliers: Positive or Negative

3-2

The person-in-charge determines if the outlier is a positive or negative leader by noticing the group's breathing when giving the outlier attention. If the group breathes low/abdominal when attention is given, the outlier is a positive leader in the eyes of the group. If the group breathes high/shallow when attention is given, the outlier is a negative leader in the eyes of the group.

If a group views an outlier as a positive leader, the group usually will look at the individual. The person-in-charge knows that whatever this individual says carries more weight in the group's mind than do the comments of a non-leader. The person-in-charge treats this individual's comments with more respect because of the individual's prestige in the group's eyes. In functional groups, the group and the person-in-charge agree on which individuals are positive leaders and which are negative leaders.

In contrast, dysfunctional adult groups mimic teenagers. If a member challenges authority, that individual is seen as a positive leader. In dysfunctional groups, the person-in-charge and the group differ on who is a positive leader. When a person-in-charge can't figure out what is occurring in a group, she can pretend they are adolescents and her clarity will improve.

Responding to an Outlier

3-3

The person-in-charge balances the needs of the group with the needs of the individual. A way to understand her balancing act is to modify the triangle of group dynamics. The top of the triangle (person-in-charge corner) becomes the fulcrum underneath a teeter-totter balancing the individual's needs with the group's needs.

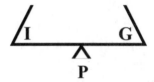

She balances by using direct acknowledgment and indirect acknowledgment strategies. The strategies are based on the non-verbal axiom that people follow the person-in-charge's eyes, but not necessarily her hand.

Direct Acknowledgment

Direct acknowledgment is when the person-in-charge looks and gestures towards the individual as she acknowledges an individual's status. For example, "At our last meeting, José cautioned us to...and his caution still applies." When the person-in-charge does direct acknowledgment, the group follows her eyes and people are likely to turn and look at the individual. Both the individual and the group recognize the acknowledgment. José's status is increased.

Indirect Acknowledgment

Indirect acknowledgment is when the person-in-charge gestures toward the person, without looking, as she acknowledges the individual's status. The person-in-charge is looking at the group in general. For example, "At our last meeting, José cautioned us to …still applies." When an indirect acknowledgment is done, the group is likely to follow the person-in-charge's eyes, thereby looking at the group in general instead of at the individual. The individual hears his name, which is satisfying, but his status in the group isn't increased.

The concept of "indirect" can also be applied to managing an inappropriate individual. When the person-in-charge manages without looking at him, the group doesn't give the individual any additional attention. In contrast, when a person-in-charge manages directly, the group then notices the individual; even though the attention is negative, it can inadvertently create (or strengthen the influence of) a negative leader.

2. Barometers[11]

3-4

In any group dynamic setting, there are individuals who are barometers of the functionality and health of the group. These individuals signal, like a pebble dropped in a pond, that larger ramifications that will follow the initial smaller circles of reactions. The person-in-charge observes how these *early responders* are reacting to what is going on, and by doing so, she knows how the rest of the group will eventually be.

Vintners plant roses at the end of the rows of grapes. The roses are more susceptible to diseases than are the grapes. If the roses look healthy, then the grapes are *safe*.

A barometer has the following three qualities:

1. The individual is a member of a subgroup.

2. The individual reacts earlier than the rest of the subgroup, and the individual's reaction is an accurate representation of how the subgroup will react in time.

3. The person-in-charge can easily read the individual's reaction.

It usually isn't possible to have barometers for the entire group. This is because as group formation occurs, subgroups emerge, each with their own leaders and barometers. Each subgroup bonds around a common value, style, or content. The person-in-charge watches the barometers of the two or three most important subgroups to read the entire group.

Since people have more than one value, people belong to more than one subgroup. In general, the important subgroups often are one of the following:[12]

- Clarity—this subgroup values understanding the concepts and expectations.

- Left-brain oriented—this subgroup follows logical, linear, and sequential presentations.

- Entertainment—this subgroup values chuckling.

- Kinesthetic-oriented—this subgroup is successful when enough hands-on experiences are provided.

- Difficult-time-grasping—this subgroup is slow to understand.

Other subgroups might be: speaking out, curiosity, higher-level thinking, fairness, skepticism, neatness/orderliness, questioning, productivity, morale, and power-brokers.

The status of any given subgroup may change over time. For example, the subgroup of skeptics might carry a lot of weight when a new boss is brought aboard. Yet three months later if the boss is doing fine, then even if the skeptics are still skeptical, the rest of the group doesn't listen to the skeptical subgroup.

Using Barometers Proactively

3-5

If the person-in-charge doesn't want the whole subgroup to react as the barometer is reacting, the person-in-charge immediately changes/adjusts what she is doing. Literally, the person-in-charge is reactive with barometers in order to be proactive with the subgroup. For example, after doing something that caused a negative response in her barometer, she takes a deep breath and steps to the side.[13] This influences the listeners to have amnesia about what happened or who did it.

3. Fostered Leaders

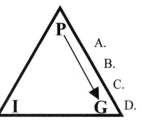

3-6

There are certain values the person-in-charge wants to be present in a group such as punctuality, curiosity, kindness and ambition. If one value, like ambition, is absent, she finds one or more unnoticed individuals who have this value. The person-in-charge fosters these members to become leaders by giving them attention. When the group members, who admire the person-in-charge, sees her giving attention to these individuals, the group tends to emulate the individuals so they can get attention also. This is the adult version of the primary teacher saying, "I like the way Philip and Janet are ready." Fostering leaders results in the group exhibiting more of the quality the person-in-charge is looking for in the group.

Vignette: Woolen Mill

Juanita was still mentally grappling with the dynamics of her office staff when she joined her friend for a three-day weekend. As she and her friend drove off for the weekend, her friend gently confronted her, "You seem preoccupied. What's going on?"

Juanita hesitantly shared that she was concerned about her advisory group. Although they were experienced, had a great sense of humor, and were excellent listeners, there was something missing. The next day, while touring the historical woolen mill Juanita made a serendipitous discovery. She found the quality she was looking for.

The guide was explaining that before they had electronic equipment with sensors, someone had to sit and watch the bolt of fabric roll off the assembly line. If the person saw a flaw, the person pressed a button that cut the blemished section. His sarcastic remark was, "Well, at least the mill found a positive use for someone who saw the glass half-empty."

Juanita hurried to work because she had finally found a useful position for her half-empty employee. She immediately summoned Becky to her office. Becky arrived with her predictable grumpy face. "Becky, I want to promote you."

Becky, "Me? Why me? You don't even seem to like me."

Juanita, "Your mind sorts for things that won't work. That talent is inappropriate for your position in customer service. But your style would be ideal for my advisory group."

4. Group Members' Identity Size

3-7

This chapter ends with a look at "Identity Size." The term "identity" refers to a person's feelings about oneself, one's character and goals; for example, a person might think "That person's identity is…" or "I identify with…." As a group becomes more formed, a "group identity" evolves.

A functional dog group will identify with the *people* at work. For a dog-oriented individual, colleagues are very important; they are like a second family. A functional cat group will identify with common *goal* of the company. For a cat-oriented individual, her success is very important.

For instance, the following graphic shows a series of circles indicating an individual's expanding levels of identity. Of course, each individual will have her own order/ priority.

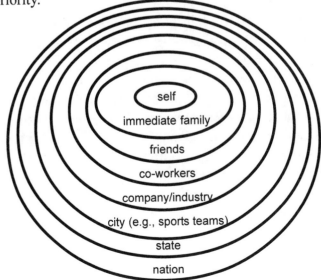

In contrast, in a dysfunctional group there is lack of identity (Chapters 5 and 6).

Vignette: Retirement Dinner

At Helena's Friday night retirement dinner, she opened with, "Thirty years ago I mortgaged everything to start our factories." Helena traced the history of their successes and ended with, "And now we are the industrial leader for the region. We have stayed small enough to have adjusted quickly in the spiral-downs. I am sure it comes as no surprise that my daughter Ola will be steering the ship starting the first of the year." The applause was more than polite—which is what Helena had hoped to hear. "Now let's be festive!"

The next morning, VIPs from the five factories assembled in the conference room. Helena opened with, "Last night was a great celebration about our past. Today is about the future. We have opened two factories in the last year and our work force has crept past the magic mark of 200—where it is harder to maintain a collective identity. As I walked the factory floor and approached people, you kindly whispered whose birthday it was and who just had a child. Thank you for making me more sensitive. This brings us to the point of this meeting." The long pause made an impact. "We are too big. We need to get back to the magic number of 200 or less. We will be dividing the factories into three divisions. Ola will walk us through the details of how this will be done."

Travel Log

Outliers

As a group becomes formed, individuals occupy certain roles. Outliers are members who are different and noticed. The reasons for being noticed change as the group evolves. Because of the attention they receive, the person-in-charge's reputation is often cemented by how she manages outliers.

The person-in-charge recognizes a group's positive leaders because the group is relaxed and breathing well when they give the leader attention. If the group is not relaxed when giving attention, then the leader is negative in the eyes of the group.

Direct acknowledgment is when the person-in-charge both looks and gestures towards the leader when acknowledging him. This increases his status in the group. If she only gestures and doesn't look at the leader when acknowledging, then the group does not increase their attention towards the leader. Often, indirect acknowledgment is enough to satisfy the individual's need for attention without increasing the individual's status in the group. The "Indirect" approach can be modified for indirect management—the managed individual doesn't increase his status when managed without eye contact.

Barometers

Barometers are the individuals who have three characteristics: they react early, their reactions represent a subgroup, and the person-in-charge can easily notice the barometers' reactions. Barometers reveal how the rest of the subgroup will be reacting. If the person-in-charge doesn't get a reaction from the barometer that she was hoping for, she can change what she is doing before the rest of the subgroup has time to react. The person-in-charge is *reactive* to the barometer in order to be *proactive* to the group.

An individual can simultaneously play more than one role in the same group, functioning as a leader, a barometer and/or a liaison (page 75). Yet in another group, the same individual might have a very different role or no role at all.

Fostered Leaders

If the person-in-charge notices that certain values are missing in the group's culture, she identifies a member who does have that value. By promoting this individual into the limelight, other members who want the same attention will emulate the individual. This fostering of the individual with the missing trait will result in a shift in the culture.

Group Members' Identity Size

By understanding how people identify with other people, the person-in-charge can predict when the group members will be close to one another and when they will be distant. This is one of the major focuses of the next chapter.

Chapter Four
Identifying Functional Cultures

Road Map

Once the group has operated for a while, the group creates its own culture. The group reveals its culture through certain behaviors.

This chapter covers four major concepts:

How to Observe—with an emphasis on "fractals"

The other major concepts are methods for identifying cultures:*

1. **Observing for leaders**

2. **Listening to a group's voice patterns**

3. **"Going to the walls"**

Once the person-in-charge knows the group's culture, that is, whether it is more doglike or catlike, then he will be able to manage more effectively and sooner.

How to Observe

When meeting with a new group, what does the person-in-charge watch for? What group behaviors will quickly give the most reliable information about the group cul-

---

To be respectful of gender equality and yet provide the reader with a fluid reading style, in this chapter the person-in-charge is referred to by male pronouns and other individuals are referred to by female pronouns.

*The longer version of this book, *Inside Track*, includes six methods for identifying cultures.

ture? Simply, how much weight does the person-in-charge assign to various observed behaviors?

The answer is found in a mathematical concept—the fractal. In a fractal, each part has the same properties as the whole. Fractal behaviors are those behaviors that appear throughout the group or even the organization. Here's how an observer determines if a behavior is a fractal:

1. Behavior occurs. Any corner (person-in-charge, an individual/subgoup, or the group as a whole) can do the behavior.

2. Observer notices the response of the other two corners. The most accurate, cross-cultural reaction to observe is breathing.

    a. If the other corners do not shift their breathing, then the behavior is typical of the group—it is a fractal.

    b. If there is a sudden change in breathing of the two responding corners, then it shows that the behavior is unusual within the culture, and therefore is not a fractal.

3. Observer assigns *weight* to observation. The observer, having observed in many different cultures, mentally has a generic set of behavioral norms. The more the fractal behavior is not found in most other cultures, the more weight the observer assigns to the behavior.

Fractal
Generic Cultural Norms (from many cultures)
Fractal

Here's an example.

> We are observing a group beginning a staff meeting. As each staff member enters and takes a seat, she turns her chair to face *away from* the boss. Neither the boss nor other group members change their breathing as people are turning their backs to the boss.

> Because no one is breathing high, we know we have discovered a fractal; this behavior is normal for this group. Compared to most cultures it is unusual for employees to sit with their backs to the boss. This is an unusual behavior, so it is given a lot of weight.

But if we were watching the same behavior in a junior high school classroom—students filing in and sitting with their backs to the teacher—we wouldn't assign much weight at all because this behavior is typical of adolescents.

Once an observer understands the concept of fractal, he can start graphing where to place a particular group. Group characteristics can be graphed by using the previously introduced axes of being issue-oriented (a cat culture) vs. being people-oriented (a dog culture).

The model of cats and dogs offers a quick, dependable way to figure out the culture of a functional group. In using the model, there are three key concepts to keep in mind.

1. Functional* dog cultures and functional cat cultures behave differently. For example, when there is con-

---

*A functional group is one where a clear purpose/style is established and followed.

flict in a dog community, it is often handled off-line. In contrast, cats in groups rather enjoy a "good go" at each other; in fact, bantering, teasing, and putting people on the spot is often the national pastime amongst cats.

Having a background in both dog and cat cultures prevents the person-in-charge from mistakenly interpreting a cat culture interaction as rude and dysfunctional and a dog culture interaction as lacking backbone and dysfunctional.

2. Knowing the degree of catness or dogness of a group allows the person-in-charge to systematically improve the functioning of any group. He realizes that progress occurs bit by bit, so he adopts realistic goals such as to:

- Move a group that is chronically dysfunctional to being only occasionally dysfunctional.

- Move a group that is occasionally dysfunctional into the functional realm.

- Add cat qualities to a predominately dog culture to move it towards "healthy."

- Add dog qualities to a predominately cat culture to move it towards "healthy."

3. A culture has to be understood before the individual member of that culture can be understood. This is because an individual exhibits behaviors from each of the many cultures of which he is a member.

When I observe a person from Guam in a mid-level management position in a manufacturing industry, the behaviors that I might see can only be understood if I have observed several people from Guam, several manufacturing work situations, and several of the people in middle management in this company. Only with this background would I be able to determine how this individual is uniquely displaying all three of those cultures. It is the blending of those behaviors makes the person unique.

When I watch myself on video footage, I can often identify which behaviors are associated with or come from which of my own cultures. If I am interviewed and asked about my relationship with my wife Gail, my face softens, my eyes get moist, and my voice becomes soft. If I am asked about my extended family, my back becomes straighter, my eyes are more steely (both proud and vigilant). When the topic changes to writing a book, my face and body becomes animated, I gesture more, I break eye contact with the interviewer, and my voice has a greater range of volume and pitch.

Identifying Functional Cultures*

There are many ways to identify the culture of a formed group. *Inside Track* presents six methods, all flowing from the metaphor of cat and dog cultures. *Fast Track* presents three of the six methods in an abbreviated form. The methods not included in *Fast Track* are: Survey for Identifying Leaders, Noticing the Speed of Interventions, and Observing Meetings.

---

*Tim Dalmau, an Australian colleague of mine, makes a clear distinction between "climate" and "culture." Tim would say that my use of *culture* equals his use of *climate.*

4-1

1. Observing for Leaders

Leaders reflect and represent a group's culture. Identify leaders by looking for two things: (1) the amount of attention the group gives to a person, and (2) how relaxed their breathing is while they are attentive. As mentioned in Chapter Two (page 49), a positive leader can be identified by observing the group doing the following:

- Members become more quiet when their leader speaks.

- They may turn their heads to look at the person.

- Members lean towards their leader when listening.

- Members adopt the phrases that their leader uses.

- Members breathe low or abdominally when listening to this person.

Once you have identified the leaders, listen to their voice patterns. Do they have a credible or approachable voice pattern?

Behaviors	Credibility	Approachability
Head	Still	Bobs
Voice pattern	Flat ———	Rhythmic ∿∿
Intonation	Curls down ⬎	Curls up ∿↗

The more the leaders have credible voice patterns, the more the group is issue-oriented, values accountability, and demands high productivity—a cat culture. Conversely, the more the leaders have approachable voice patterns, the more the group is people-oriented, values acceptability, and seeks high morale—a dog culture.

Travel Tips—Observing Baselines

When observing during a meeting, the members might be listening because of the speaker's position of authority. In this case, he observer would have to observe the group at several meetings and watch the group's baseline listening style with several individuals of equal positional status. Then when the group is more attentive than usual, the observer can calibrate that the group looks up to the individual, apart from the individual's position.

Dogs and cats listen very differently. Remember to take this into account when observing to identify the group's leaders. For example, a dog-oriented member will nod whenever anyone speaks, so an observer would need to establish a baseline of a dog member's nodding. Once the baseline is established, then an increase in that dog member's nodding means the dog supports, agrees with, and/or looks-up-to the current speaker more than the other speakers. Since a cat almost never nods, even a slight nod from a cat could be significant.

Vignette: The Next Factory

Arriving home, Sally listened to her voice mail. She recognized the voice of Anita Chemeketa, the head of a factory.

The next morning Sally arrived at Chemeketa's office. Chemeketa opened with, "As you know, Sally, my counterpart at another factory was very pleased with your insights about his staff and your recommendations on how to optimize his leadership.

Chemeketa continued, "Every group, like a snowflake, is unique. Yet you quickly and consistently know how to identify the group's leaders. Tell us how you do that."

Sally explained that she was trained in non-verbal communication as well as group dynamics, "If appropriate, I could sit in on meetings and identify your leaders and write up a report estimating where the staff collectively is along with some recommendations.

Two weeks later, Sally presented her report. "Observations at the meetings revealed that all department heads are respected leaders except the maintenance chief, Shawna. With the exception of Shawna, whenever the department heads talk to their own group, people are silent. They all breathe comfortably and are at ease with offering their opinions. The one concern is that the departments don't trust each other enough. We need to develop some liaisons; that is, we need people who are respected cross-departmentally. That's my first recommendation. With your permission I can observe some more and figure out whether you have invisible liaisons that need to be brought into the light are or if you need to hire them."

Sally continued her report. "The second recommendation would involve a change in the maintenance department. When Shawna was conducting her bi-weekly meetings, half of the members wouldn't even make eye contact with her. And when they did look at her, they began to breathe even higher. She is an ineffective bully—her crew fears her but they don't respect her. And she isn't comfortable being a boss...she stumbles over her words. A good way to explain what is occurring is to use an equestrian metaphor. A rider can do anything to a horse—even whip it—if the rider is comfortable with himself. But if the rider isn't comfortable, the rider releases certain odors. When a horse smells these odors, the horse won't let the rider get on its back, even if that means the horse will get whipped again. Shawna is the rider and the group is the horse. They don't trust her. They passively resist her. The more they resist her more the she whips, resulting in their increased resistance.

Chemeketa, "Sally, your observations are right on target—you have put words and specifics to what I have sensed also. Let me think about it for a week."

2. Listening to a Group's Voice Patterns

4-2

Most groups operate with a collective sound that can be identified as credible, approachable, or a blend. The more the culture of the group is "issue-oriented," the more the sounds will remain flat or credible. The more the culture of the group is people-oriented, the sooner the approachable voice patterns emerge.

An issue-oriented group is drawn to a culture of:	A people-oriented group is drawn to a culture of:
focus on issues	focus on people
aim for high productivity	aim for high morale
conclusions	processes
answers	dialoguing
short, succinct statements	longer, more vulnerable statements

4-3

3. Going to the Walls

This, the last method for identifying a group's culture, may be the most interesting. A quick background on how it came about will increase your appreciation of the method and its potential benefits.

The longer I have worked in non-verbal communication, the more fascinated I have become with creating useful, generic, all-purpose templates. A template is generic if it can be applied cross-culturally. For example, the concept of cat vs. dog voice patterns (credible cats having flat voices that curl down at the end of phrases and sentences, and approachable dogs having rhythmic voices that curl up at the end of phrases and sentences) is only useful if it can be flexibly applied to many cultures. An inflexible application would be to say that Northern Germans are all credible-oriented because of their cultural voice patterns or that all Mediterranean cultures are approachable because of their cultural voice patterns. A flexible application of voice patterns would be the following:

1. First establish the cultural norm.

   a. Compared to other European cultures, Northern Germans have a credible voice pattern.

   b. Compared to other European cultures, Mediterranean cultures have an approachable voice pattern.

2. Only after the norm of a culture is established can we understand where an individual fits in that culture.

   a. For example, the Northern German who has a hint of a rolling voice is accurately detected to be more approachable then other members of the same culture.

   b. Similarly, the Mediterranean individual who has a hint of flatness of voice is accurately detected to be more credible than other members of the same culture.

3. Cross-cultural comparison must be done with caution.

   a. The Northern German who is more approachable than his mates still has a flatter voice than the credible member of the Mediterranean culture.

   b. Likewise, the Mediterranean individual who is more credible than his mates still has a more rolling voice pattern than the approachable member of the Northern German culture.

   c. Cultures tend to misinterpret each other because they are sizing up the other person from their own cultural norms. The Northern German is mistaking the Mediterranean individual with a flatter than average voice pattern as being approachable because the Northern German is using the lens of the Northern German culture. He doesn't understand that in the Mediterranean culture, this individual is actually acting credible.

To bypass my own ethnocentric lens, I invented an activity called Going to the Walls. It is a process whereby members identify each other's degree of credibility or approachability on a on a five point scale. The scale is flexible in that, instead of having just two categories of credible and approachable, the gradations between them are fleshed out. Here is how the activity works:

1. The group needs to know most members. If they are a formed group and already know each other, it will take me three hours to teach the basic concept of credible and cat vs. approachable and dog, and then we can begin the voting.

2. We have signs on opposing walls of the training room. For purposes of orientation, let's say the East wall has the sign "credible" on it. The West wall has the sign "approachable" on it. For gradation purposes, the Northeast corner has the sign "credible with some approachable." The Northwest corner has the sign "approachable with some credible." The North wall has a sign, "50-50."

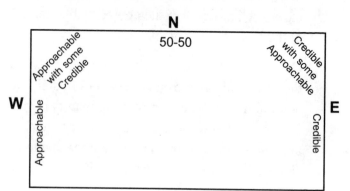

3. The group votes. Each person takes a turn standing with their eyes closed. The instructor asks, "How many see this person as more credible-oriented?" The instructor counts or scans the room for the votes and then says, "How many see this person as more approachable-oriented?" The instructor has the person open his eyes and indicates which of the five locations to go to. After several people have been voted on, the instructor reduces the questions to, "credible?" and "approachable?"

4. Subgroups discover commonalities. After everyone has been placed in the five locations, each location is broken into subgroups of 3-7 people. Each subgroup is given a flipchart paper with a marker. They put the name of the location at the top of the paper. They discuss and list things they have in common, including values, attitudes, beliefs, and axioms they live by. The next step for each group is to list any additional commonalities (such as region raised, religion, level of education, careers, birth order).

5. Once the flipcharts are completed, the instructor gives the following suggestion to the large group. "The values listed in the five locations reflect the span of cat and dog cultures. One person from each subgroup will read their paper aloud to the large group. Notice how new values and beliefs appear as we move from one wall to another wall. And watch how the values, beliefs of one wall often disappear by the time we get to the opposite wall."

Having done "Going to the Wall" on three continents, I am convinced that the values that appear in each of the five locations in Germany are the same values that appear in the corresponding locations in America and Australia. However, each value (for example, "loyalty from subordinates," on the Credible list) plays out very differently in the German's hierarchical society compared to the Australian's egalitarian culture. The Germans interpret "loyalty" as something that is demanded because of one's position, whereas the Aussies interpret "loyalty" as something that is appreciatively expected and earned via fairness. One of the most shocking discoveries is that an individual can only be understood after one understands the culture that the individual is a member of.

> *Culture precedes the individual.*

The following is a list of the most common values from three continents. We have only listed the three walls; the two corners are a mixture of the two adjoining walls.

Credible	Liaison	Approachable
takes charge of	broker/mediates	in-service to
efficient	friendly w/reservations	outgoing/friendly
impatient w/ incompetence	balanced	humble
directs well	processes well	listens well
independent/self-sufficient	flexible	interdependent
demands evidence	depends on situation	assumes honesty
structure/rules for others	can switch roles	follows structure/rules
"It's up to me"	forge alliance	"It's up to us"
systems oriented	earned leadership-oriented	relationship oriented
purpose-driven	facilitates success	likes relaxed atmosphere
high expectations	realistic / adaptable	high relationships
demanding	balance	accommodating
go it alone	collaborative	with familiar others
likes new challenges	flexible	likes routines
knows best	balanced	defers easily
leadership	team w/leader	team
definitive	synergy	empathic/caring/gentle
big brain	body-mind	big hearted
makes the rules	rules = guidelines	play by the rules
honesty	diplomatic	kind
time is constant pressure	balance deadlines & people	laid back
productivity	harmony w/limits	morale
guttural voice	raises questions	soft spoken
visionary	"why/how" combination	can carry out
BIG EGO	changes with situation	team ego
accountability	wants both	acceptance
determined/tenacious	loves to learn	wants to follow
visual-oriented	a blend	oral-oriented
communicates by position	combination	communicates by person
intervenes quickly	thoughtful	intervenes slowly
pilot	based on circumstances	flight attendant
control	depends…	cooperative
likes accomplishment	both	likes appreciation/liked
will listen to others but still decides	outputs based on inputs	consensus

"Going to the Walls" reveals how the members think about themselves individually and collectively. Several insights are:

1. It is fascinating that the extreme walls will both claim certain traits such as flexibility, openness, responsi-

bility, loyalty, commitment, self-improvement, hard work, integrity, quality, trust, optimistic, dependability, develop people, communicative.

2. Equally fascinating is how the two extreme walls view the opposite wall. For example, dogs see cats as stressed out, arrogant, and pushy; cats see dogs as under-ambitious, humble in an ineffective way, and wimpy.

3. Each of the five groups has its own culture.

4. Each of the five groups has an easier time communicating with the group immediately adjacent to them than with those who are one culture removed. The cultures in the middle each have two other cultures with which they can easily communicate. The extreme walls have only one culture they can easily communicate with.

5. Extremely credible and extremely approachable individuals inside an organization are likely to feel isolated and misunderstood. What is true of individuals can be extended to subgroups. If an accounting department is located at an extreme wall (for example, the credible location), then the whole department will tend to feel isolated and misunderstood. And the projected judgmental views mentioned in number two above will apply to everyone in the department.

6. The more a group or an entire organization is extremely credible or extremely approachable, the more prone the group or organization is to be occasionally dysfunctional.

The Value of a Liaison

4-4

When there is an absence of people voted to the 50-50 wall, the group/organization is in trouble. The title and role of the members on the 50-50 wall is "liaison." There is a direct correlation between the health of a group and the number of liaisons present.[14] Whenever a group splits into camps, the likelihood of dysfunctionality increases. The presence of liaisons prevents a group from splitting into camps. For a functional group to become a healthy group, the most needed variable is an increase in liaisons.

A liaison is seen by some colleagues as being committed to, and motivated by, productivity. This same individual is seen by other colleagues as committed to, and motivated by, morale. Literally, a liaison has membership in multiple subgroups. A liaison is an ambassador between groups. The liaison is welcome in subgroups and can explain to that subgroup another subgroup's values and perceptions.

Travel Tips—Liaison

As persons-in-charge, we practice the strategies to foster individuals into liaison roles. In those groups where we are not the person-in-charge, the fastest way to increase our value to the group is to increase our own liaison profile. A liaison has a range of behaviors. By selecting the behaviors and values that are appropriate for a given situation, we become charismatic liaisons. The difference between a charismatic leader and a charismatic liaison is that the charismatic leader has positional power.

The best way to prepare for being a charismatic leader is to practice being a charismatic liaison. As a liaison, we don't have authority, so we have to figure out how to accomplish things in other ways. We form wonderful habits:

1. We ask ourselves, "If I don't have permission to do what needs to be done, who does?" I approach that individual. This teaches humility and that our own ego needs to be in control for us to be effective.

2. And if I don't have permission to broach the needed strategy with the individual who can get it done, then I ask, "Who does have permission to approach that individual?" That's the individual I approach. This teaches me group dynamics—people's titles are not the same as their sphere of influence.

3. And one final caution: liaisons go unrecognized and under-appreciated, and they are usually not candidates for promotion (page 137). So when we are not the person-in-charge, we have to be clear with ourselves. We have to decide which is more important to us: being promoted or being the hub that makes the wheel go around. If being promoted is more important, we will have to operate more from our catness. If being the hub is more important, we will have to operate with greater flexibility. Either answer is acceptable.

4. When we are the person-in-charge, we must remember to appreciate liaisons. At the same time, we must be careful about promoting them because they sometimes lose their ability to be the hub

when they are promoted. Perhaps find some way, other than promotion, to show appreciation.

Travel Log

Chapter Four focuses on identifying the culture of a variety of functional groups. The culture is revealed by the *fractal* behaviors that are typical of the group dynamics. The person-in-charge identifies the culture of a formed group so the person-in-charge can facilitate and manage effectively. Functional groups span the whole range from an all dog culture to an all cat culture. The culture of a group is revealed through the leadership of the group. Three methods of identifying leaders, and thereby the values of the group, were offered:

1. Observing for Leaders

An option for identifying leaders is to observe which individuals are given positive (e.g., relaxed breathing) attention. Then use the voice patterns to identify which values the leader has—which reflects the group's values.

Behaviors	Credibility	Approachability
Head	Still	Bobs
Voice pattern	Flat ———	Rhythmic $\wedge\wedge\cup$
Intonation	Curls down ⟶	Curls up $\wedge\wedge\cup$

2. Listening to a Group's Collective Voice Patterns

A second alternative is to attend meetings and listen to the collective voice pattern used by the group. Then use the voice patterns in the previous chart to identify which values the leader has—which reflects the group's values.

3. "Going to the Walls"

This last method offers the widest array of information and is designed to avoid cultural bias; letting the group identify or categorize all members,

The members of a known group are asked to identify each member as being either "credible" or "approachable." Based on how the group voted, each member then goes to one of five locations that are gradations of credible and approachable.

In "Going to the Walls," each person receives feedback on how they are seen by others. And by directing each group to list their values (beliefs, attitudes, axioms they live by), the whole spectrum of values is revealed.

The Value of a Liaison

A liaison has membership in several subgroups. There is a direct correlation between the group's health and the number of liaisons. If there is a shortage of liaisons, either foster them or hire them.

You are invited to read *Inside Track* for three more methods of identifying the culture of a group.

Chapter Five
Occasionally Dysfunctional Groups

Most functional groups and individuals experience occasional dysfunction. This explains why TV shows such as *Everybody Loves Raymond* are so popular—we see aspects of our own family portrayed in the dysfunctional TV family. We all have dysfunctional luggage. Some of us are able to reduce it to a "carry-on." Even with baggage, functioning groups can carry on with their purpose.

Road Map

Fast Track offers a continuum of groups from healthy to functional to dysfunctional.

This chapter looks at the variables that can influence functional groups, whether doglike or catlike, to become temporarily dysfunctional. Groups at the extreme ends of the functional line are more prone to temporary dysfunction than are those closer to the center. For example, a people-oriented group that operates near to the center axis has some cat traits. They are less likely to experience occasional dysfunction. Likewise, an issue-oriented group that operates near to the center axis has some dog traits. They are less likely to experience occasional dysfunction. Those groups that are closer to the center have a balance of both cat and dog traits and are less prone to temporary dysfunction.

To be respectful of gender equality and yet provide the reader with a fluid reading style, in this chapter the person-in-charge is referred to by female pronouns and other individuals are referred to by male pronouns.

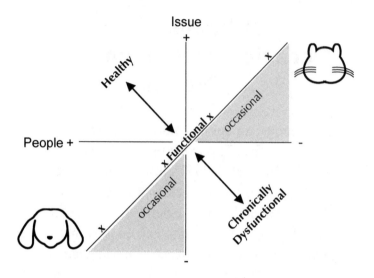

A dog group becomes dysfunctional when the premium put on the individual becomes overextended and unbalanced. When the individual is all that matters, the group shows the following characteristics:

- Egalitarianism is misunderstood; there is no positional power.

- How each individual perceives is more important than how the group perceives.

- The culture is one of "the individual is all that matters."

- Elephants are present: either they are invisible or if someone does speak of their favorite elephant, others don't voice their perspective.

- Reality is stopped if one person isn't okay.

- Consensus is needed before the group can move forward.

- The person-in-charge will accommodate again and again, then suddenly implode (or explode).

A cat group becomes dysfunctional when the premium put on productivity and results becomes overextended and unbalanced. When results are all that matters, the group shows the following characteristics:

- Hierarchical is misunderstood; power gives you the right to be selfish.

- How the group perceives justifies steam rolling over individuals.

- The culture is one of "getting results is all that matters."

- People say what they think, regardless of whom it might offend.

- Those who can bully their way are given free rein.

- Position is seen as permission.

- Stress is constant and burnout is high.

Cultures are like forests. The more diverse the forest, the more resilient the forest will be. A functional dog culture with cat members is less likely to become temporarily dysfunctional than is a functional group that is all dogs and no cats. The same is true for a functional cat culture; having dog members increases the group's resiliency. Diversity, when accepted, balances the culture.

There are seven variables* that influence a functional group to become dysfunctional. These variables don't nec-

---

*Instead of "variables" some researchers would prefer "Probability Density Function."

essarily mean that the group *will* become dysfunctional; it depends on the person-in-charge, the individual members of the group, the group as a whole, and the system the group is a part of. The seven dangerous variables that the person-in-charge of a functional group monitors are:

1. **Norms and Surprises**—when the group is surprised.

2. **Stages of Irritability**—when the group is annoyed.

3. **Seasonal Dysfunction**—when launching a new project, product, or protocol.

4. **Gender Misinterpretation**—when the speaker misinterprets the non-verbals of the listener.

5. **Positional vs. Personal Compliments**—when a compliment is misinterpreted.

6. **Directional Communication**—when an individual operates differently when interacting with a peer, people above, or people below and others misinterpret.

7. **Favoritism**—when the group perceives the person-in-charge likes certain members.

Potential Causes of Temporary Dysfunction

5-1

1. Norms and Surprises

Most people are drawn to and operate well when routines and norms are followed. Routines include protocols, schedules, expectations, goals, and timelines. Routines make their lives more predictable. There is comfort in predictability.

Unexpected events can cause mental and emotional disturbances. The group tends to dip into being dysfunctional. There are three variables that influence the extent of the damage: duration—how long the uncertainty lasts; intensity—the severity of the surprise; and frequency—how frequently the surprises occur.

The degree of damage cause by an unexpected event is based on the norm that the group is used to. For example, emergency personnel responding to a fire will have a very different reaction from that of people who live or work in the building that burned. When surprised, a functional group tends to become dysfunctional. Just *how* different the surprise is from the group's norm influences how dysfunctional the group might become.

The signs that a group has been surprised in a negative way are easy to spot; people pull their heads back, breathe high and look straight ahead. Negative surprises cause the group to become instantly unformed, or, more accurately, instantly dysfunctional.

Travel Tips—Being Familiar

As observers, if we are familiar with the culture we are likely to be emotionally calm and accurate in our assessment of the group's level of surprise. If we are not familiar with the culture, we are likely to be less calm and less accurate in our assessment of the group when we ourselves are surprised.

A veteran primary teacher visiting a middle school classroom might be traumatized if a fistfight breaks out. The veteran middle school teacher handles his emotions much better than does the visitor from elementary school. Yet when that same middle school teacher visits the preschool classroom and a student throws up, the visitor might not be able to get the picture out of his head when eating dinner that night. Meanwhile, the veteran preschool teacher is enjoying her meal at home.

Vignette: Rookie Reporter

As a new journalist Adrian Adrenalin talked her boss into doing a "ride-along" with the fire department. By the second night, Adrian was getting comfortable with sleeping at the fire station—that is, until the siren interrupted her slumber. By the time the blaring engine arrived at the two-story building, her body was twitching from the adrenalin rush.

Four hours later she sat soaked in sweat on her bunk bed. She had never been so simultaneously exhausted and yet unable to sleep. The next morning, she sat wearily staring at her computer. She realized that all her impressions were just that —"her impressions." On the phone she begin her apology, "Boss, I don't know what to say. I don't have a story."

He responded kindly, "Overwhelmed with excitement?" His understanding soothed Adrian. She began to relax as he continued, "You are sane. Stay with it. After a few more ride-alongs, you will get your bearings and be able to start observing. You have good instincts—we just have to train them."

2. Stages of Irritability

As a group becomes formed, the members get to know each other. They know each other's habits, traits and idiosyncrasies. It is natural for members in a functional group to become irritated by certain members' styles. Sharing space in a limited environment increases the likelihood of getting on each other's nerves.

If the irritableness between members is limited and the group can function, the person-in-charge probably can let the individual members work it out. But if the group's functionality is in question, the person-in-charge intervenes.

This section focuses on recognizing and effectively managing the first two stages of irritability: shocked (surprised) and confused.

> ***Surprises are seen as unfair.***

There is a third stage, annoyed, which will be dealt with in the next chapter (page 118).

5-2

Each of the stages of irritability has a sensory specific description of the group dynamics pattern. The person-in-charge uses this evidence to identify the stage and then respond appropriately.

When an unformed group initially perceives an individual as inappropriate, the group is momentarily shocked. The room gets very quiet as heads go back, people breathe high, and everyone looks straight ahead. When the person-in-charge sees these signs that the group is shocked, the best way to manage the situation is to respond gently.[15] This is because the group thinks that how the per-

5-3

son-in-charge treats the inappropriate individual is how she will treat everyone.

5-4

If the individual continues with the inappropriate behavior, the group enters the second stage: confused. When the group is confused, members pull their heads back and hold their breaths—in addition, their foreheads will furrow and they will turn slightly toward each other as if to say, "Do you see this situation the same way I do?" Now, the group sees things differently, and how the person-in-charge manages these individuals will in no way indicate how she would treat the rest of the group. The group wants to get on with the business at hand. The individual is being seen as holding up the group. Responding gently is no longer appropriate. The next chapter (page 102) addresses how the person-in-charge changes when responding gently is no longer effective.

When the group is in the confused stage, the person-in-charge has an obligation not only to the individual corner of the group dynamic triangle, but also to the group corner. If the person-in-charge cannot satisfy both corners, then the best strategy is to err on the side of satisfying the group.

Vignette: "Take him straight on."

Arielle had been living her dream of being the board chair for three months, but now the honeymoon was definitely over.

Hank, the spokesperson for three of the eight board members, had increased his criticism of the direction she was advocating. Arielle was used to being tested. But Hank wasn't testing. He was throwing roadblocks in her way.

She phoned Basil, her mentor of yesteryear, and arranged a coffee conference. Arielle and Basil shortened their usual social "catching up" and moved to the professional reason they had met. Basil listened calmly and interspersed questions.

After forty-five minutes, Basil began, "You are sophisticated in applied group dynamic techniques. You realize the board is a split group and you have applied the appropriate techniques of bonding the board (EASY, page 35). You have tried to see Hank 'off line' to handle his pettiness. This would be an appropriate strategy if the group were functional. When a board is dysfunctional, and currently they are, you have to operate from a different toolbox. Go into meetings and isolate Hank. Take him straight on. Let the minor split become a gaping chasm. Trust that the functional members will side with you."

"Remember two things: the more dysfunctional the group, the stronger your role of person-in-charge must be. And secondly, as soon as the group shows signs that they are moving in the direction of being functional, switch out of your power posture."

When the person-in-charge is part of the group from its inception, she can easily chart the progression of the group's reaction from one Stage of Irritability to the next stage. However, if she enters an environment where the dynamics are already set, it is likely that the group is already shocked or confused by one or more individuals. Knowing the physiological indicators of the stages allows her to match her response to the stage the group has progressed to.

When the group is shocked or confused, *management* is called for. The purpose of management is to keep the individual as a member of the functioning community. When the group is annoyed with an individual member, *discipline* is called for. The purpose of discipline is to keep the group a functioning community by isolating the individual. Any time the person-in-charge disciplines an individual, the potential for the group becoming dysfunctional increases. This is why "Annoyance" is covered in Chapter Six (page 108).

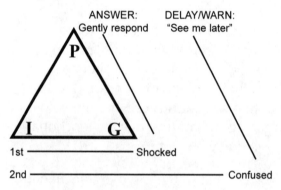

```
        ANSWER:        DELAY/WARN:
      Gently respond    "See me later"

          /\
         /P \
        /    \
       /      \
      /        \
     / I     G  \
    /_____\
1st ──────────── Shocked
2nd ───────────────────── Confused
```

Physiological indicators of stages:

        Shocked:
        • head pulled back
        • breath held

            Confused:
            • head pulled back
            • breath held
            • furrowed forehead
            • slight turning toward
              each other

5-5

3. Seasonal Dysfunction

Chapter Three introduced the concept of "identity size" (page 55). Seasonal Dysfunction expands that concept.

In functional groups, especially on routine days, members identify with one other (page 55). All functional groups have *seasons*; that is, they have times when there is a change in routines and people either increase or decrease their identity with other members of the group. The person-in-charge must be aware of seasonal situations that influence a functional group to become dysfunctional.

The evidence that members identify with the group as a whole is found by listening to the collective voice volume when the group is assembled. When the members are doing group work and the collective volume of voices in the subgroups remains at or below a certain level, it's an auditory sign that the subgroups identify with each other. Some high identity examples:

- The office is busy with people keyboarding. From time to time, one or more of the 15 members may need to turn and interact with another member. When several subgroups are all talking at the same time, there is an even hum of productivity.

- The Girl Scout troop has divided into units of three. Each unit is rehearsing their forthcoming skit. As one unit increases their volume, the other units might have a tendency to also increase their volume, but in this case they don't get louder.

Each of the above groups might have a different collective volume. For instance, decibel levels at the Girl Scout rehearsal have a higher ceiling than those of the office groups. But if each group maintains a certain ceiling, the person-in-charge can assume that the subgroup members not only identify with the members in their immediate unit, but also with the collective group as a whole.

5-7

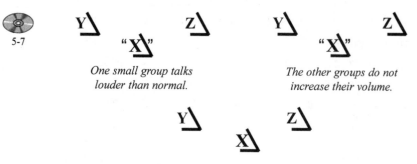

One small group talks
louder than normal.

The other groups do not
increase their volume.

The "X" returns to collective norm.

Changes in routines may affect the group's identity size. Sometimes a change in routines results in a decrease in identity size—this is seasonal dysfunction. People's sense of identity with the group shrinks from "all of us" to "my closest associates and me." And sometimes, simply to "me." When this occurs, the group's ability to function is decreased. This evidenced by an increase in the noise level of the subgroups.

5-8

Changes in routines include simple things like a change in weather (e.g., first snowfall, first spring sunshine). Re-organization and reengineering almost certainly affect people's identity size. The seasonal change affects different members of the group (and system) differently; this is especially true when intense time pressure is present. From Girls Scouts having the push for their cookie drive, to a corporation being in the final phases of launching a project, protocol or product deadlines tends to exacerbate fatigue and bring about a shrinkage of identity circles.

Before a predictably tough season starts, an effective person-in-charge calls a meeting and thanks people ahead of time for the pending season's demands on everyone. Thanking people after the group has weathered a storm wears thin.

Vignette: "Thank you."

Amy genuinely appreciated the staff that worked for her. Her fulfillment company experienced seasonal ebbs and flows. At the end of a particularly hectic season, she treated the staff to a nice lunch. Everyone enjoyed Amy's professionalism in honoring them. Amy started off with, "Frank, you had to stay after several nights to box the next day's shipment. Sally, you had to drive across town twice to pick up supplies. And Mohammad and Tess, your willingness to coordinate the shipping company pick up helped us meet our deadlines."

By the time Amy had hosted the third luncheon, however the impact of appreciating the staff was not as effective. That is when she decided to switch her appreciation meetings to before the storm started, "I want to thank everyone ahead of time. Frank, you know it is coming—the extra hours necessary to box the next day's shipment. Sally, keep your car filled with fuel (ha ha) 'cause the cross town drives are going to be needed. And Mohammad and Tess, your rolodex will be spinning as you coordinate everything so we can meet our deadline."

In reflection, Amy discovered that the post storm appreciation didn't outweigh the exhaustion, whereas the pre-storm appreciation wasn't competing with any fatigue.

Years later, Amy was a guest lecturer for an MBA program. She started her talk, "Proactive vs. Reactive Appreciation" by asking, "Raise your hand if you have given birth to a baby. The sheer joy of seeing, hearing and holding your child outweighs

> the labor you just endured. But work is not like childbirth. Your employees at work are different. They want to be positively reinforced *before* the labor."

Sometimes members change their identity circle because of a change in their level of responsibility. For example when a project is coming to an end, different levels of the group (and system) experience a decrease or an increase in their levels of responsibility. For example, if upper management puts in longer hours than middle or front line people, the potential for the sections not feeling unified increases; the likelihood of the group becoming dysfunctional increases. The classic example is when management is salaried and the front line is unionized (paid by the hour and restricted to certain hours per week). The group tends to split into camps of "us" and "them." When sections of a group experience different levels of responsibility the section with the lower level of responsibility becomes:

- More short-term oriented,

- More impulsive,

- Less left-brain linear and more right-brain creative,

- Less able to concentrate, and

- More egalitarian and less authoritarian and hierarchical.

This causes those with higher levels of responsibility to go through the stages of shocked, confused, and annoyed (page 108).

The suggestion is for the person-in-charge to interact with members using the following strategies.

Decrease	Increase
Interactions between sections that are experiencing different levels of responsibility.	Interactions between sections that are experiencing the same levels of responsibility.
Oral communication	Visual communication
Reliance on authority	Reliance on rapport
Reliance on the individual	Reliance on the group (EASY, page 35)

4. Gender Misinterpretation

5-6

Deborah Tannen and others have increased the public's awareness that genders communicate differently.[16] The differences between men and women's communication styles are great enough to be considered "culture." When people are unaware of the differences between the genders, the misinterpretation is likely to lead functional people/groups to be at least temporarily dysfunctional. A person-in-charge can often explain the gender differences to people so that the misinterpretation is temporary and the communication returns to being accurate and functional.

When a boss listens, statistically the subordinate associates certain styles with the gender of the boss. In general, the credible voice pattern is associated with the male and the approachable voice pattern with the female (page 64).

The following chart summarizes the statistical ways that the subordinate interprets the boss.

Speaker's Gender	Listener's Gender	Listener's Style	Speaker's Interpretation of Listener
male	male	male	= processing the info
female	female	female	= following the info
male	female	female	= "She could be agreeing, and yet I could be mistaken."
female	male	male	= "He may not be agreeing or following, and yet I could be mistaken."
male	male	female	= wimp, pushover
female	female	male	= offended, abandoned
male	female	male	= cold, sterile
female	male	female	= sensitive, new-age guy

5-7

5. Positional vs. Personal Compliments

An interesting side note to "Gender Misinterpretation" is the concept of compliments. When a boss gives a compliment to a subordinate, it can be done with the credible voice or with the approachable voice. If it is given with a credible voice, then the subordinate is receiving the praise from the boss' *position* and not from the boss *personally*. The following are axioms regarding compliments and voice patterns:

- Initially the male can be motivated by compliments from the boss' *position*.

- The female is more motivated by compliments from the boss' *person*.

- The longer someone works for another, the greater the subordinate is motivated by the *person* giving the compliment.

A person-in-charge can mentor bosses to be aware of how their compliments might be received. A person-in-charge can guide bosses to give a compliment that will most likely increase the recipient's motivation. When there are misunderstandings, she can also explain how recipients may have misinterpreted the compliments and misunderstood what the boss meant to communicate. Clearing up misinterpretations returns communication to a functional level.

6. Directional Communication

5-8

The person-in-charge's style of communication often is contingent on the *direction* toward which is communicating.

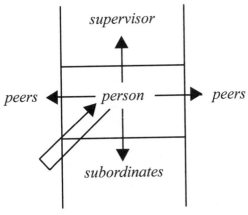

A person-in-charge communicates and manages in four directions: upward to bosses, downward to subordinates, sideways to colleagues or within to herself. And for each direction, there may be a different style. If the person-in-charge doesn't recognize this surface level of inconsistencies in herself and others, the person-in-charge will mistakenly interpret the behavior as dysfunctional.

Usually an individual is consistent in each direction. For example, a person-in-charge could be consistently kind and compliant to her bosses and consistently demanding of subordinates, while consistently ignoring colleagues.

Since *Fast Track* is about managing groups, the most important direction is how the person-in-charge views herself when managing others, whether that is managing up (bosses), down (subordinates), or laterally (co-workers). Simply, how comfortable is she when managing?

How would a person-in-charge know her own (and others') comfort level when she is managing (or immediately following her managing)?

The observable evidence of a person's comfort level is the person's breathing. If someone is breathing low/abdominally, the person is comfortable. If someone is breathing high/shallow, the person is not comfortable. There is an important distinction; sometimes it is appropriate for the person-in-charge to breathe high when managing, such as being angry at an unruly situation. In this case, it isn't how the person-in-charge is breathing when managing, it is how fast she recovers following the management. Does the person-in-charge retain the emotions after the management is over (continues to breathe high/shallow and is uncomfortable) or does she somewhat have amnesia (decontaminates,[17] breathes lower and regains comfort)?

Since looking at a person's chest to detect low and high breathing is socially awkward at the least, it is more appropriate to look at the indirect by-products of low and high breathing.

Indirect Indictor	Low Breathing = Comfortable	High Breathing = Uncomfortable
When talking	Can find words; fluid	Can't find words; "um"
When moving	Fluid	Jerky
When reposing	Still	Stiff

Travel Tips—Meta-emotional*

The above chart illustrates the observable evidence of comfort. We can also use an internal model. How we feel when managing is important—do we feel comfortable? But even more important is how we feel about how we feel.

For instance, we can ask ourselves, "How do we feel when managing?" If we feel disappointed, hurt or angry when managing, we probably don't welcome those emotions. We probably don't feel comfortable when managing. But, if we ask ourselves, "How do we feel about feeling disappointed, hurt, or angry," and we do feel justified in feeling these emotions, then we are comfortable after the managing. We will recover quickly.

> *It is not how we feel that matters.*
> *It is how we feel about how we feel.*

A person-in-charge's lack of comfort with managing others can cause dysfunctionality. The more uncomfortable a person-in-charge is when managing others and the more frequently the person-in-charge has to manage, the more severe the dysfunctionality. Chapter Seven addresses the

---

*How one feels about how one is feeling is called meta-emotional.

need for a person-in-charge to select the culture that fits her level of comfort. If an individual is promoted or hired into a culture that is beyond her comfort level, the person-in-charge can be the cause of the dysfunction. This explains a very simple fact. People don't want to work for a person-in-charge who will not cover their back from inappropriate pressure from bosses, will not hold co-workers accountable or will not support their handling of inappropriate subordinates.

> *People want to work for someone who buffers pressure, holds peers accountable and supports their handling of inappropriate subordinates.*

And they don't want to work for someone who won't support how they handle their own inappropriate subordinates.

5-9

7. Favoritism

People-in-charge have always known that showing favoritism towards certain members has the negative consequence of splitting the group. The person-in-charge may consciously try not to show any hint of partiality, but on the unconscious level she can't help but reveal how she feels about certain individuals in the group. Her face, voice, body posture/proximity and breathing continually communicate degrees of like or dislike. For example, when a person-in-charge calls on a worker for business purposes, the person-in-charge physically comes closer to the worker she likes than to the worker she dislikes. The reverse is also true. When the person-in-charge calls on a worker for corrective or disciplinary purposes, she stays farther away from the worker she likes and moves closer to the worker she dislikes.

Travel Log

This chapter describes the seven variables that influence when functional cultures tend to become dysfunctional. These variables don't necessarily mean that group will become dysfunctional; it depends on the person-in-charge, the individual members of the group, and the group as a whole.

1. Norms and Surprises

Most people are drawn to and operate well when routines are followed. Routines are the norms that people are use to. Unexpected surprises cause mental and emotional disturbances and can be the basis for the group becoming dysfunctional. The more the person-in-charge can decrease surprises, the more likely it is that the group will remain become functional. It is essential that the person-in-charge not be surprised when the group is surprised. When she can see "it" coming, she is not surprised.

2. Stages of Irritability

A formed and functional group is initially "shocked" at an inappropriate member; if the member persists, the group becomes confused. A person-in-charge takes her cues from the group's stage of irritability to prevent the group from becoming dysfunctional. It is critical that the person-in-charge be seen as fair when managing the individual.

3. Seasonal Dysfunction

When sections of a group experience different levels of responsibility, members expand and contract their identity with each other. When the seasonal level of identity is low, the group is more likely to become temporarily dysfunctional. When the person-in-charge knows ahead of time what is likely to happen, she switches to her pilot persona and starts the EASY process.

4. Gender Misinterpretation

Men and women have different communicating styles. The more the styles are different, the greater the chance for misinterpretation and dysfunction. The person-in-charge can act as a liaison between styles to decrease possible misinterpretation.

5. Positional vs. Personal Compliments

The purpose of the compliment is to motivate the recipient. Different people are motivated by different styles of compliments. When the person who sends a compliment has a style very different from the style of the recipient, the likelihood of miscommunication increases. A person-in-charge can mentor people on how to effectively give compliments.

6. Directional Communication

A person-in-charge's comfort in managing in a variety of directions (e.g., bosses and subordinates) is essential for the group to function. Low breathing is evidence of "comfort." A smart person-in-charge selects the culture that fits her level of comfort. People want to work for someone who buffers pressure, holds peers accountable, and supports their handling of inappropriate subordinates.

7. Favoritism

The person-in-charge clearly distinguishes between professional and personal reactions to individuals. The sorting has to be in keeping with the culture of the group. This habit of separating the professional and the personal will prevent favoritism and dysfunctional treatment of individuals. An unbalanced group (too "dog" or too "cat" oriented) increases the likelihood that a group will become dysfunctional. Above all, the person-in-charge should work to keep the functional group balanced with a mixture of dog and cat traits.

> *Diversity, when accepted, balances the culture.*

Notes

Chapter Six
Chronically Dysfunctional Groups

"Happy families are all alike.
Each unhappy family is unhappy in its own way."
Tolstoy[18]

Road Map

Once dysfunction becomes the norm, the group's culture reinforces the dysfunctionality. Dysfunctional groups either don't have a clear purpose or cannot carry out their purpose. Habits and traditions perpetuate themselves. Chapter Five presented seven variables that influence a group towards temporarily dysfunction. Over time, what was temporary becomes chronic. The nine variables in Chapter Six have a more negative influence on groups than do the seven variables in Chapter Five. The amount of influence of the variables described in Chapters Five and Six is based on the Duration, Intensity and Frequency of the negative variables.

This chapter first discusses the role of the person-in-charge, then presents the nine variables that increase the likelihood of chronic dysfunction.

––––––

To be respectful of gender equality and yet provide the reader with a fluid reading style, in this chapter the person-in-charge is referred to by male pronouns and other individuals are referred to by female pronouns.

The Role of the Person-in-charge

The person-in-charge's role with functional dog groups, functional cat groups and with healthy groups is:

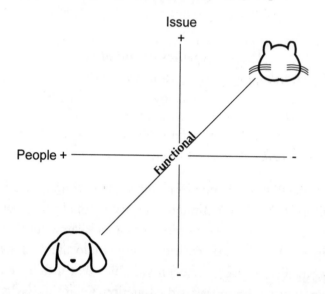

The person-in-charge's role with a chronically dysfunctional group is very different. Here are some of those differences:

6-1

Management vs. Discipline Strategies

The recommended strategies for functional and healthy groups need to be modified and sometimes scrapped for dysfunctional groups. For example, Chapter Seven will recommend the management method[19] for dealing with controversy, volatile topics, and negative news as:

- Posture yourself at 90°.

- Sort your communication into two categories:

- Positive information, the relationship level of the communication, and the solution

- Negative/volatile information, the issue level of the communication and the problem

- When dealing with the volatile issue/problem, use a third point and have the option of speaking in a credible voice pattern.

- When dealing with the positive information, the relationship, and the solution, use a second point and speak in an approachable voice pattern.

With dysfunctional groups, the person-in-charge has to train himself to look the individual or the group in the eyes and very calmly indicate what is expected and what will happen if the inappropriate behavior continues.

Travel Tips—Congruency

There are five non-verbal behaviors that we develop in order to be an effective person-in-charge of a dysfunctional group. We combine all of these non-verbals in any disciplinary communication:

- Keep our body still, especially our head.

- Talk with slow, deliberate gestures.

- Pause frequently.

- During the pause, freeze the gesture until we start to talk again.

- Breathe from the abdomen. This is critical.

These non-verbal behaviors increase our congruency. When we are congruent, people are very impressed.

Our belief is transferred to them. In addition to the five non-verbals listed above, there are two advanced congruency techniques that are especially powerful when we want to move people:

- While maintaining eye contact, deliver the most important part of the message without blinking. Blinking detracts from our congruency. When our eyes remain open, the message is perceived as a whole unit—not open to negotiation. This especially works with big cats. While the big cat might interpret it as a stare-down contest (which is what boxers do to each other while the referee is explaining the rules), our calm breathing defuses that impression. Once the cat blinks and we don't blink, the cat becomes more respectful of us.

- The second skill is delivering the most important part of the message in a whispery voice. This keeps the recipient's metabolism calm. They hear us better and are less likely to react impulsively.

With functional groups, the person-in-charge manages. The purpose of management is to keep the individual(s) a member of the community. The person-in-charge can anticipate immediate or eventual compliance.

With dysfunctional groups, the person-in-charge disciplines. The purpose of discipline is to isolate the individual or subgroup so that the larger group can move towards being functional. Discipline is necessary when the person-in-charge cannot anticipate eventual compliance. (See page 118, Annoyed Stage, for details on this concept.)

> *We manage functional groups.*
> *We discipline dysfunctional groups.*

Travel Tips—Below the Line

In essence, the rules of engagement above the functional line are different from those below the functional line. When we operate above the functional line, our instinct is to use *permission* as a framework and operate with influence. "Power" is reserved as the back up alternative. When operating below the functional line our instinct is to suspend the concept of permission; we gather as much authority as possible and operate as a power pilot. As the group starts to improve, we consider switching to some influence.

Different Rules of Engagement

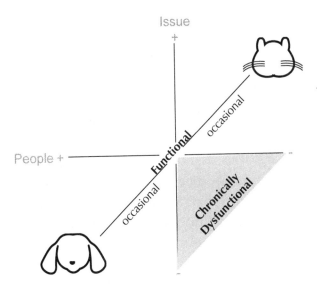

6-2

Split Groups vs. Cohesive Groups

With functional groups, the person-in-charge wants the group to be cohesive. He will use the four techniques of EASY (page 35) to build and maintain the group's cohesiveness.

With a dysfunctional group, the person-in-charge will intentionally split a segment off from the dysfunctional majority and work to make that smaller section functional. This is why a person-in-charge disciplines; he disciplines to create a beachhead of functionality. The people who immediately experience the sanity of the functionality will become the person-in-charge's biggest supporters.

A worker experiences health, functionality, or dysfunctionality most vividly through the colleagues she rubs elbows with. It is her immediate contacts that determine if her work environment is healthy, functional or dysfunctional. Chapter Eight will address how "group health" and "functionality" are experienced (page 210).

6-3

Pilot and Energy

An unformed group and a dysfunctional group warrant use of the same strategy by the person-in-charge. A person-in-charge who has inherited a dysfunctional group will initially operate the same way he would operate with an unformed group. In both situations, the person-in-charge starts off as the pilot (page 34)—he is in charge of agenda, goals, etc. Operating as a pilot means that the person-in-charge is more positional than personal. This consumes more energy because the person-in-charge doesn't get to be himself at work.

The difference between the person-in-charge of an unformed group and the person-in-charge of a dysfunctional group is the length of time the person-in-charge stays pilot. The person-in-charge of the unformed group can apply EASY strategies (page 35) and be optimistic that in time the group will become formed and the person-in-charge can switch to a flight attendant mode. Whenever the person-in-charge can be more himself, less energy is expended.

In contrast, it is likely that the person-in-charge of the dysfunctional group will need to remain positional indefinitely. In order to not expend as much energy in the positional mode, the person-in-charge over time identifies more and more with the pilot mode. As the pilot style becomes more comfortable, more a part of who he is, he expends less energy at work. Most career people who work with dysfunctional groups develop a crusty surface so that their emotional heart is protected.

Drill sergeants whip raw, unformed, dysfunctional recruits into a cohesive unit. But the military system can only let an officer do so many rotations as a drill sergeant before it has to give him a different assignment; otherwise, the officer runs the risk of developing a jaded, caustic (bossy, know-it-all, obnoxious) outlook that becomes a 24/7 lifestyle. For another example of how a dysfunctional population affects the person-in-charge, Google Karpman Drama Triangle.

As the person-in-charge of a dysfunctional develops the habit of always acting from position rather than person, his work gets easier, but his home life gets more difficult. Why? Because the person-in-charge has a tendency to make the crusty surface a lifestyle. As an example, the divorce rate for people in law enforcement is usually higher than it is for people in other lines of work.

Vignette: Caretaking

I was sharing the differences between the person-in-charge of a dysfunctional group and an unformed group with a neighbor who kept nodding her head and saying, "Tell me about it!"

I finally said, "You are retired. How would you know about these ideas?"

With steely eyes she said, "I am the middle generation of caretaking. I am visiting my mother every other day, and at least three times a week I watch my two-year old grandson, Luke.

"When I visit my mom, I am not optimistic. Sure, she has some good days and is coherent—we get to reminisce, but overall she is not progressing."

I momentarily lapsed into thought, "She is describing dysfunctional groups."

She continued, "When I am watching Luke, I probably work even harder than when I am visiting Mom. Luke is into everything. I am constantly either preparing food, changing diapers, or cleaning up after him. And yet, there is an optimism—every week there is progress as he grows more and more responsible and independent of me."

As I listened to her description of toddler-care, I sat stunned by how parallel it was to the optimistic care with which a person-in-charge leads an unformed group. And her description of caring for her mom parallels the pessimistic work of a

Explaining is unnecessary.

person-in-charge of a chronically dysfunctional group.

Travel Tips—Decontaminate Our Home

If we work with dysfunctional people, we want an effective way of separating work and home. We might be effective at work in our ability to handle pressure, reduce stress, and solve problems. This is our positional persona. But we are loved at home because we are personal, present, and vulnerable. This is our person persona. Our decontamination of work and home is essential for our health.

When we are home and being our person, we are off duty. We recharge our batteries. This is why we need to keep the non-verbals of our work contained in one spot at home. For instance, putting our brief case out of sight (in a closet, in a study, behind a chair) removes the constant reminders of our obligations. It is especially important to keep reminders of work away from where we eat and sleep.[20]

Expectations:

6-4

Of course, it would be great if our dysfunctional group were part of a functioning system. Then we could count on appreciation from above. And the system could assist us with realistic expectations. *Fast Track* suggests that when we work with functional groups, success can be measured by "the results we get." When we work with dysfunctional groups, however, success is measured by "how we did based on the level of receptivity we were able to gain." Usually a dysfunctional group's gains are not as great as those of a functional group. When we have the good fortune to be part of a functional system, the system will remind us of our own sanity and value even if our dysfunctional group does not.

We might find ourselves in a situation where we are brought in to turn a dysfunctional group into a functional group. Sometimes we can lead the group into becoming functional and sometimes we can't. Often we are not the sole determinant of whether we can be successful. And even if we do remove the dysfunctional elements, we are often seen as such a "bad guy" that we have to be replaced with a new person so that the functionality can be stabilized.

6-5

Vignette: "...a few selective funerals."

"Hacket" Harriet earned her nickname by being sent to any dysfunctional branch that the global headquarters deemed necessary. She usually was able to "clean house" in eighteen months.

Luckily, her husband Jack liked to travel and, as a novelist, he could work from anywhere. Besides, the diverse locations provided grist for his writing.

Harriet and Jack's ritual was to stop all talk about work at the end of dinner. When they did talk, Jack privately made mental notes on her process for "branch cleaning." She would have liked to just observe for two to three months, a practice which she could do with functional groups.

But with a dysfunctional group, she inherited crisis and had to make decisions immediately. During her second week, she returned home with a look that Jack responded to by saying, "Let's eat out tonight!"

With candlelight and over a slow glass of fine wine, she shared her day. Jack listened with a knowing look and an empathetic nod of his head. Respectfully he offered, "Sounds like the observing stage is over. I admire how you continue to handle crisis after crisis, and yet you also continue to observe."

Harriet, "Jack, you know it is because of your acceptance of me that I am able to work in an environment where I don't care if I am liked or not." Then, with a curious voice she asked, "Now tell me, how do you know I can do that?"

Jack leaned closer, "When you tell me how different people and departments are responding to you, you are talking from your own, healthy self."

After a few more sips, she teased, "So tell me, what does your crystal ball reveal about the next stages of my house cleaning at this branch."

"Well, dear, if the pattern holds true you will need at least three months to determine which departments are capable of being functional, and you will invest most of your energy in supporting them. These departments will start becoming functional. Then you will spend the next half year figuring out which other departments and VPs know that you are not playing favorites. You are reinforcing the behaviors you demand. The functioning departments will be rewarded with increased attention from you."

Harriet, "Am I that transparent? Wow, I completely agree with you! So what happens next?"

> Jack, with a twinkle in his eye, "Remember Donald Walker's book, *Never Try to Teach a Pig to Sing...Wit and Wisdom for Leaders?*[21] One line in it reminds me of the next stage in this job. Walker said something like, 'Most organizations could benefit from a few selective funerals.'"
>
> Harriett was laughing enough that Jack took the poetic license to add, "Funerals put the fun back in dysfunctional! Think about it: the 'dys' is a sleight-of-mouth way of saying, 'Dies.' Hey, get rid of the 'dys' and you are functional again."

Anyone working with a given population is likely to enjoy gallows humor. It is only understood by colleagues. The laughter releases tension. If someone outside the professional heard the joking, they would think that the professionals are insensitive and callous. So too, people who work with a dysfunctional populations develop a humor that would seem dysfunctional to people outside the given profession. Maintaining a slightly irreverent sense of humor is healthy. (You just have to be selective in choosing with whom you share it.)

Performance Criteria

Mission and vision statements can motivate functional groups. A subordinate can be evaluated based on how she is carrying out these statements. Often an employee is assessed as meeting or not meeting certain standards. This "either-or" system is often preferred by the dog culture; meeting the standards confirms membership in the pack, and dogs love inclusion.

An alternative to the "either-or" approach is the rubric approach. The rubric approach describes levels of competency, with each level having its own specific, observable indicators. The rubric approach can move a functioning culture into a healthy culture. Rubrics inspire ambitious (a cat trait) employees to continually grow more competent, and they provide a blueprint for accommodating (a dog trait) employees to be even more efficient. A healthy culture is an environment that encourages life-long learners.

With a dysfunctional group, it is fruitless to communicate in abstractions such as mission and vision statements. They need specifics. With dysfunctional groups, lofty statements have to have nitty-gritty descriptions of behaviors (much like rubrics) that are expected and required in order to realize the mission and vision statements. It is fine if there is more than one behavior to get to the same lofty goal.

Background

In general, when a person-in-charge is mentoring or coaching functional people, it's okay to share similar personal experiences; oftentimes, sharing similar experiences bonds people together. The person being assisted feels like the person-in-charge can identify and understand her. However, the person-in-charge needs to guard against thinking that he understands what the person is sharing simply because he has had an equivalent experience. If someone says, "My father died last week" and if the listener then searches for an equivalent loss in his own experience, the listener may mistakenly assume that he knows what the other person is feeling. This assumption—"I understand what you are feeling"—can be wrong, and it can annoy or insult the speaker. In contrast to using this "faulty empathy," the effective listener tries to learn what the death means to the speaker.

When the listener is really listening, the speaker gets to share what the death means to her. For example, if the listener thinks of when he lost an aunt to whom he was very close, he is assuming that the speaker is grieving, whereas the speaker might be relieved that her parent's long-term illness is finished and he is no longer in pain. She may be relieved of the responsibilities of caring for her aging parent.

This listening strategy (not sharing similar experiences) works well with functional people, but it doesn't always transfer to working with dysfunctional groups. For instance, when working with addicts, it is very helpful to have a similar background—such as being a recovering addict. Why? This is because these clients have sophisticated denial patterns that the average person-in-charge can't detect. The clients could be pathological liars; only someone with a similar experience could see through their clever lies and hold the clients' feet to the fire.

> *The effective strategies for functional groups are not necessarily transferable to dysfunctional populations.*

A person-in-charge of a dysfunctional group may not have a similar background; in this case, he can be schooled in techniques that will work with these groups.

For example, someone who works in a counseling capacity with deviant youth can be taught not to look at the client, because eye contact can activate chemicals of aggression.

In contrast, someone who works with the same deviant youth but in a management capacity (for example, as a guard) might never break eye contact.

Potential Causes of Chronic Dysfunction

1. Dysfunctional Meetings

6-6

Chapter Five presented the concept that dysfunction cannot be defined in isolation. A dog visiting a functioning cat culture leaves thinking, "This group is dysfunctional!" A cat visiting a functioning dog culture leaves thinking the same. A dysfunctional meeting has many of the following features:

- The culture has an unclear focus: is the focus on productivity, issues, and accountability? Or is the focus on relationship, morale, and acceptance? Or neither? Nobody knows.

- Members are at different phases of the decision-making process: some are gathering information (dogs) while others are deciding on information (cats) (page 212).

- Stress is high, as evidenced by their high/shallow breathing.[22]

- The group can't stay on topic. They cannot keep a detached, objective view of the topic under discussion. The group is beyond facilitation and management. What is needed discipline.

- And most important, the person-in-charge lacks the power to punish the cats that are out of control, and without this disciplinary power in their leader, the dogs are unsafe.

> *We can manage with influence.*
> *We discipline with power.*

6-7

2. Annoyed Stage

In Chapter Five (page 85), the concept of two Stages of Irritability was introduced. When an individual (this would be true also for a subgroup) is persistently inappropriate, a formed group progresses through three Stages of Irritability. The evidence of each stage is summarized in the following graphic.

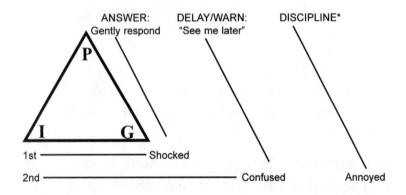

Physiological indicators of stages:

Shocked:
• head pulled back
• breath held

Confused:
• head pulled back
• breath held
• furrowed forehead
• slight turning toward each other

Annoyed:
• sounds made
• full turning to look at each other

---

*Discipline has consequences. Management is preventive discipline.

When a functional group is shocked or confused (the first two Stages of Irritability), management is called for. The goal is to keep the individual as a member of the functioning community. If the individual persists in the inappropriateness, the group transitions to the third stage—annoyance. When the group is annoyed, discipline is called for. Discipline differs from management in that discipline has consequences. The purpose of discipline is to keep the group a functioning community by isolating the individual.

The person-in-charge has to have power to impose the disciplinary consequences. If he doesn't have the support from the system (pages 192-210), he is unable to be the pilot the groups needs him to be. Without support from the system, he will not be effective, and the potential for the group becoming or remaining severely dysfunctional will increase.

Ignoring—The Fourth Stage

If the person-in-charge doesn't have the organizational support to use discipline, his best option is to teach the group to ignore the individual using an ignoring technique such as Indirect Acknowledgment (page 49). The purpose of ignoring an individual isn't necessarily to get compliance from the individual but rather to confirm the sanity of the group (page 188). A person-in-charge can also decrease an individual's status. The strategy for decreasing status is to create noise when an inappropriate individual is about to talk. Because people intuitively associate increased noise with annoyance, the individual's status is decreased.

6-8

6-9

3. Individual As Bully

The presence of one or more bullies in a group increases the probability that the group will become dysfunctional. When a group is annoyed with a bully, they dare not make sounds because they fear retaliation from the bully. Instead, the group silently rolls their eyes and people quickly exchange glances with neighbors as if to confirm, "We're all seeing it the same way." Instead of counseling a bully, consider the following:

1. If possible, remove or fire the bully. (For cautions, see Rumors, page 121.)

2. If you can't remove the bully, then isolate the bully using the Ignore technique (page 119).

3. Remember to appear fair to the group. You don't have to appear fair to the bully.

4. If a dysfunctional group has been beaten into silence by the bully's verbal intimidation, switch from oral communication to visual communication. Historically, this was the purpose of secret ballets. A modern equivalent of the secret ballot is "Electronic Response System" voting. The voting works in the following manner:

    A list of topics and positions is generated. A meeting is held and the statements and questions (which have been typed into a computer) are projected onto the screen/white board. Each member has a remote voting device (the size of a TV remote). Everyone votes and the tallies are instantly revealed on the board. The votes can be either anonymous or identified by the voter. In either case, the silent dogs' votes are just as powerful and valid as the vote of the bully cat.

Verbal tabulation or input gives cats disproportionate advantage because either they are articulate or they don't care whether or not they are articulate. Converting the voting process to a visual input system allows the dogs to participate fully because their input-can be anonymous. With the dogs safe, the group gets an accurate picture of how the group sees the situation—the bully is in the minority. The group becomes more functional because the voting has confirmed the group's sanity.

4. Adolescents and Fairness

6-10

In a functional culture, the group and the person-in-charge tend to agree on which individuals are positive influences and which individuals are negative influences. In a chronically dysfunctional culture, however, it is more likely that the group will view an inappropriate individual, who is clearly a negative influence, as a positive leader. In fact, the more bizarre the individual acts, the more status the individual receives from the group. This is often the case with teenagers. Therefore, when the dynamics of a group are not making sense, pretend they are adolescents.

The person-in-charge is fair when two conditions are met: (1) the group perceives that the individual has been publicly warned that a consequence is coming, and (2) the person-in-charge is seen as consistent.

5. Rumors

6-11

A corollary to Adolescents and Fairness is Rumors. Rumors occur when the person-in-charge tries to keep the process of disciplining an individual private. Although the manager's motivation is positive by trying to respect the privacy of the individual, the strategy might backfire.

The person-in-charge determines whether to discipline privately or not by asking himself, "Is the inappropriate individual likely to comply with my warning?" If the answer is "Yes, the individual will probably comply," then it is beneficial to the group's concentration that the discipline be done in privately.

If the answer is "No, the individual will probably not comply with the warning," then the group benefits from being aware that some disciplinary process is occurring. Why? Since the group is aware that the person-in-charge is disciplining the individual, the group will not be surprised if the individual is demoted or fired. The person-in-charge doesn't want the group to be surprised because surprise causes dysfunctionality.

Another complication occurs when the inappropriate individual, who being privately disciplined starts spreading rumors about how the person-in-charge is being unfair to the individual. Since the group doesn't know that the person-in-charge is privately disciplining the individual, the group might believe the individual. When the person-in-charge finally has to expose the discipline, the group is likely to be shocked and believe what the individual had be saying about the person-in-charge. As Suzette Elgin says, "False perceptions have real consequences."[23]

Here is an example of how to indicate to the group that an individual is being privately disciplined. As the meeting ends, while members are closing their notebooks and computers, the person-in-charge says loudly enough for the group to hear and in a not-open-for-negotiation voice, "Frank, please stay after." The meeting adjourns and the group members file out while the person-in-charge talks privately to Frank. The members out in the hallway are abuzz speculating on what is happening inside the room.

6. Pushing a Group

6-12

Pushing a group spans all the chapters of *Fast Track*. When a group is unformed (Chapter One), the members depend on the person-in-charge to provide the safety for the group; that's why the person-in-charge cannot push an unformed group. The person-in-charge uses the EASY techniques (Chapter Two) to form the group.

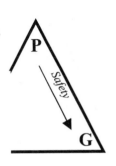

Initially person-in-charge provides the safety.

In Chapter Three, the group is formed and has started to provide their own safety. The person-in-charge can't push yet, but he can start to expect more of the group.

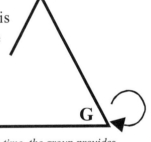

In time, the group provides their own safety.

Chapter Four presents the idea of functioning cat cultures and functioning dog cultures. The person-in-charge's wisdom is in understanding the fact that what is expected of a cat group would be interpreted by a dog group as pushing. The person-in-charge who understands the idea of dog and cat cultures is able to predict how different groups are likely to respond to high expectations and pushing.

Chapter Five indicates that if the safety is no longer provided by the group (for example, because of seasonal shrinkage of Identity Size), the person-in-charge has to return to providing the safety.

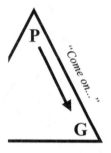

Person-in-charge pushes group.

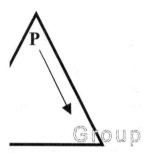

Group's Identity Size is shrinking.

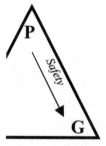

Person-in-charge stops pushing and starts providing safety.

Chapters Four to Seven explain how certain groups might react to being pushed: they either stay functional, become temporarily dysfunctional, become chronically dysfunctional, or become healthy.

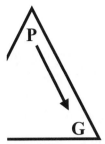

The person-in-charge can push/demand more of the group.

The group grumbles amongst themselves yet meets the new demand level.

Travel Tips—Provides Their Own Safety

On the surface, we weaken our relationship with people when we push them. But here is the secret! Instead of the person-in-charge having "high relationships" with the group, he arranges for the group to have high relationships with each other. If group members have high relationships with one another, then we can push them.

The evidence that the group has high relationship with each other is that when they feel pushed by the person-in-charge, they look at and talk to each other. Sometimes they even complain about the person-in-charge…the group is providing their own safety. And yet they fulfill his demand.

In contrast, if group members don't look at each other when they are pushed and instead look down at the floor or up at the ceiling, then the person-in-charge can't push them because they are not providing their own safety. The person-in-charge has to provide the group's safety.

Pushing a Group is in this chapter because if the person-in-charge persists in pushing a group that is not providing their own safety, the culture can become chronically dysfunctional.

6-13

7. Victim

This variable is based on Herb Cohen's concept of the three variables of negotiation: Power, Information and Time.[24] Functional individuals and groups operate either "win-win" (the outlook of dogs) or from "win-lose" (the outlook of cats). A person-in-charge can successfully negotiate with either. In contrast, dysfunctional individuals and groups tend to operate from "lose-lose," a victim approach. The victim actually wants the person-in-charge to attempt to reach her because then she has the secret satisfaction of getting back at the person-in-charge by passively withholding information and time. Picture a scene where a parent wants to talk to her teenager. The first thing the teen says is, "How long is this going to take?" (= withholding time). This is quickly followed with "Can I go now?" (= withholding information). The parent may have the power card, and yet, the teen is holding the other two cards of information and time.

A person-in-charge needs to recognize the *symptoms* of the victim and consider which, if any, of the *strategies* that follow might work.

> *When working with a chronic dysfunctional*
> *individual or group, the person-in-charge*
> *has to keep his own sanity.*

Symptoms

Each of us has a persona inside that is a victim. This persona surfaces during adolescence. There are several indicators that a person is in a victim mode:

- She withholds information and time.

- She feels sorry for herself.

- She feels bad and wants others to suffer also.

- She wants "freedom from…" instead of "freedom to…."

- She is emotionally reactive instead of proactive.

- On one level, she wants to have someone in authority explode at her because that proves how others pick on her. As much as the individual resents the person-in-charge having power over her, the victim doesn't want to be empowered.

Strategies

Strategies for working with a group or person in temporary victim mode:

- Point to the rules/expectations in silence.

- Make sure that you are breathing well and emotionally okay; ignore any words or ploys that would tend to hook[25] you.

- Watch for times when the individual is not in her victim role and brainstorm a plan of action of how she wants to act and be treated during her "temporary victim" time.

- Stay at 90° (side-by-side) with the individual and avoid eye contact.

- Don't pursue her. Figure out how to have her come to you.

- Understand that the victim hates pressure to do well. For example, know when to use "encouragement" instead of "praise."[26]

- Keep looking for opportunities to develop a relationship with the person, because it is through positive contact that she develops hope.

- Try to let the person select choices within the guidelines that the person-in-charge sets.

6-14

8. Accommodate, Accommodate, Explode

If the person-in-charge repeatedly uses power inappropriately, the group culture can become chronically dysfunctional. An example is his tendency is to be overly accommodating. The concept of accommodating spans a whole range of descriptions. At one extreme, it can mean the person-in-charge is flexible and can change his expectations to accommodate the request from an individual or the group as a whole. At the other extreme, "accommodating" includes situations when the person-in-charge is not respected/appreciated by cats. If the person-in-charge repeatedly accommodates and tolerates "disrespect," each incident is like the proverbial straw that is laid on the camel's back, with the person-in-charge being the camel. Over time, the "straws," accumulate. If the person-in-charge continues to accommodate, he is likely to explode[27] when the final straw breaks the camel's back.

If the group has witnessed only the final straw, they might agree that the person-in-charge was disrespected, but they are mystified at the intensity of his reaction. The people are stunned because the explosion seems out of proportion to the specific incident that occurred. They are likely aware of the single straw, but not the collective weight of all the straws the person-in-charge was responding to.

A dog-oriented person-in-charge has to resist the temptation to apologize after exploding. The cycle of exploding and apologizes results in group dynamics schizophrenia.

Travel Tips—Different Season

To avoid the Accommodate, Accommodate, Explode." cycle, *Fast Track* suggests we do the following:

1. When managing, we remain dissociated.

2. Manage early, before we feel.

3. Develop our cat part and manage from it.

4. Manage when the *group* needs it (not when *we* need it).

5. And most importantly, stay fit to avoid fatigue. And when fatigued, don't operate from our intuition. Colin Powell said this about seasonal fatigue, "Moments of stress, confusion and fatigue are exactly when mistakes happen. And when everyone else's mind is filled or distracted, the leader must be doubly vigilant."[28]

6. Decrease surprises. Surprises are the enemy of competence.

> **Surprises are the enemy of competence.**

When we do find ourselves surprised by a situation, we review what happened and figure out what were the early signs that we missed this time sbut will see in the future.

When a person works with a dysfunctional population, he is affected by this population. He has to be careful not to become dysfunctional also. If you work with this population, Google "Karpman's Drama Triangle."[29]

9. Asocial Individual

The expression that "one bad apple can spoil the whole barrel" applies to group dynamics. The person-in-charge observes not only the individual but also the group reaction to the individual. In this section, two scenarios are offered. In the first scenario, the individual is temporarily asocial and in the second scenario the individual is chronically asocial.

6-15

Temporarily Asocial Individual

An individual is acting in such a way that the group is actively annoyed. The difficulty is that the individual is temporarily unaffected by the peer pressure. The person-in-charge recognizes that the individual is willing to socially self-destruct. Later, the group may not easily forgive the individual member for how he acted, so it is better for the person-in-charge to step in and manage the individual and not let the group give the person their input.

This intervention is best done before the group moves from the *confused* stage to the *annoyed* level. The person-in-charge can only save an individual if the person-in-charge intervenes before *annoyance* sets in.[30]

Chronically Asocial Individual

6-16

The group perceives that an individual consistently acts inappropriately. The individual is immune to group pressure and the person-in-charge cannot establish a relationship with the individual. Consequently, the person-in-charge has to use power instead of influence. The person-in-charge's obligation is to try to remove the individual because the collective group health is at stake. If he cannot remove the individual, he teaches the group to ignore the person.

Travel Log

The Role of the Person-in-charge

The person-in-charge of dysfunctional groups knows how to switch from managing to disciplining. The strategies for managing a functional group don't work with a chronically dysfunctional group. In order to stay healthy, the person-in-charge has to take care of himself both at work and at home.

The nine variables that increase the likelihood of chronic dysfunction are:

1. **Dysfunctional Meetings**

   Dysfunctional meetings have two traits: participants are in high stress and the group doesn't follow the person-in-charge.

And most important, the person-in-charge lacks the power to punish the cats that are out of control, and without this disciplinary power in their leader, the dogs are unsafe.

2. Annoyed Stage

When the group switches from being confused to becoming annoyed, the person-in-charge switches from managing to disciplining. Discipline has consequences. The person-in-charge has to have the backing of the system (his bosses) to carry out consequences. If he can't remove the individual, he teaches the group to ignore her. The technique of artificially creating noise when the individual is acting out reduces her status. The group functions in spite of the individual.

3. Individual as Bully

A bully is someone who has annoyed the group but they are afraid of her. The person-in-charge has several choices: remove her, isolate (ignore) her, discipline her while being fair in the eyes of the group, and/or use an "Electronic Response System."

4. Adolescents and Fairness

When a person-in-charge is confused by the behavior of dysfunctional adults, he can pretend he is dealing with adolescents—then everything will become clear. He suspends the concepts of Stages of Irritability and uses straight discipline. Appearing fair, which is being consistent and warning people that a consequence is coming, is critical to helping the group become more functional.

5. Rumors

A person-in-charge's reputation is often based on his professional judgment as to whether the inappropriate individual will comply. If he thinks "yes, the individual will comply," then he handles the discipline privately. If he thinks "no, she probably will not comply," he has to indicate to the group that a disciplinary process is underway. This way, the group won't be surprised if the consequence becomes public.

6. Pushing a Group

Instead of the person-in-charge having "high relationships" with the group, he arranges for the group to have high relationships with each other. Then he can push the group to higher productivity because they will care for each other. There is a caution: if he pushes the group and they don't look at each other and instead look down at the floor or up at the ceiling, then he can't push because they are not providing their own safety. Pushing a group like this will cause the group to become chronically dysfunctional.

7. Victim

When individuals or groups are dysfunctional, they display the following traits:

- They withhold information and time.

- They feel sorry for themselves.

- They feel bad and want others to suffer also.

- They want "freedom from ..." instead of "freedom to...."

- They are emotionally reactive instead of proactive.

- They hold to a self-fulfilling prophecy that says, "Authority picks on me."

While strategies are offered for dealing with the dysfunctional group, it is even more important for the person-in-charge to be realistic and take care of himself.

8. Accommodate, Accommodate, Explode

The person-in-charge is not above being the cause of the dysfunctionality. One example is when the person-in-charge is too dog and falls into "accommodate-accommodate-explode" cycle, and then makes it worse by apologizing for exploding.

9. Asocial Individual

This short section examined the different strategies the person-in-charge selects based on whether an individual is temporarily asocial or chronically asocial. The strategies are based on the concern for the group and how they are responding to the individual.

Chapter Seven
Healthy Leaders, Healthy Groups

The person-in-charge of a healthy group is a leader—a wise veterinarian who has realistic expectations of dogs and of cats. A healthy group is a humane society.

Road Map

All road maps lead to this and the next chapter. In this chapter "Health" is presented in two major sections:

1. Leader's Traits and Self Care

A person-in-charge can be healthy without the group necessarily being healthy. If the person-in-charge is healthy, the chances are greater that the group will be healthy. The chapter answers questions such as:

- What are the traits of a healthy person-in-charge and how do we develop them?

- When can we trust our gut reactions? How do we educate our instincts so that they are accurate more often?

- How do we, like a healthy person-in-charge, review our day so we will have more options for the next time a similar situation arises?

To be respectful of gender equality and yet provide the reader with a fluid reading style, in this chapter the person-in-charge is referred to by female pronouns and other individuals are referred to by male pronouns.

- How do we, like a healthy person-in-charge, take care of ourselves and manage our energy?

2. Management—The Key to a Healthy Group

Because *Fast Track* is a management-focused book, the primary focus is on specific ways to create a healthy work environment, one with high productivity and high morale.

There are key principles and strategies to healthy management:

- Recognize how the group is viewing a situation.

- Use only the appropriate amount of power.

- Accept that stereotyping will occur amongst members, then lead members beyond their own limiting beliefs to become full, multi-faceted humans.

- Share the leadership with members.

- Confirm the sanity of the group when dysfunctional members can't be removed.

7-1~2

Leader's Traits and Self Care

The traditional image of "leadership" laps over into "charisma" which includes charm, physical attraction, confidence, and competence—a commanding presence. Ian Fleming made a career of portraying "Bond, James Bond" as such a person. *Good to Great* debunks this stereotype; in reality, the combination of consistency, vision, and leadership trumps wit, strength and charm.

Below are *Fast Track's* eleven traits of a healthy person-in-charge. But first, there are three cautions:

1. While the list does provide a checklist of behaviors for the reader to consider, it is admittedly idyllic.

2. If you are a cat in a high issue-oriented culture, and have a high level position, you might not be interested in developing all these traits for yourself. The adrenalin rush from stress may invigorate you. However, what a great list to use for interviewing, hiring, and promoting the liaisons that you need immediately below you.

3. If you are a dog in a people-oriented culture, you might enjoy the hospitality of donuts and coffee and not want to develop all these traits for yourself. You might like the high acceptance that your current position offers. However, what a great list to use for seeking a person-in-charge that you want to work for.

Traits of a healthy person-in-charge:

1. A healthy person-in-charge has a conscious competence. Whether or not she uses the language of *Fast Track*, she can recognize group dynamic patterns, and she has a wide range of responses.*

2. She exhibits many of the traits that appear in functional cultures:

    Dog traits: accepting, approachable (weight not evenly distributed, joints bent, voice sounds friendly—curls up, palms up when talking, rhythmic movement, rhythmic gestures people-oriented, good listener (bobs head and makes encouraging

*On our web site (www.michaelgrinder.com) there is a cognitive review in the form of a study guide for *Fast Track* patterns.

sounds), empathetic, lives by the Golden Rule (treat others the way you want to be treated), acknowledges birthdays, asks people about what's important to them in their private world, egalitarian, appreciates people, asks instead of tells or demands, wouldn't presume or assume, less formal (speech, dress, behaviors), values popularity, likes to gather information, operates from a personal level. Can facilitate people, and can seek consensus.

Cat traits: values accountability, credibility (weight evenly distributed, joints straight, voice sounds "business-like"—curls down, palms down when talking, body more still, staccato gestures), issue-oriented, good speaker, when listening can easily interrupt, acknowledges accomplishments, hierarchical, appreciates issues, presumes and assumes, could be formal (speech, dress, behaviors), definitive, sends directives well, lives by the Platinum Rule (treat others the way they need to be treated), deadline driven, values power and authority, knows what is best for others, Likes to decide, operates from a positional level. Can manage people, and can give orders.

3. She can recognize and respond to the following groups:

   - Unformed group—forms them via pilot style

   - Functioning dog group—facilitates

   - Functioning cat group—manages

   - Dysfunctional group—stays with power piloting

- Healthy group—leads

4. She understands that the group comes first, especially during difficult times.

5. She understands norms and has good timing; she knows when to be within the norms and when to be outside (page 142).

6. She shares leadership by transferring her relationship with individuals to relationships amongst members (page 151).

7. Her first preference is to operate from *person*. At the same time, she is able to recognize when the situation calls for *position*, and she can easily shift to power (page 152).

8. She is comfortable with systematic inconsistence; she operates from set principles (page 153).

9. She has an educated unconscious in that she knows when to trust her instincts and when not to. This is because she knows how to review and reflect on her day; she keeps learning (page 154).

10. She has good timing in that she uses the appropriate level of power until the inappropriate party starts to shift to Neutral.

11. She realizes the critical importance of timing for increasing her permission to lead the group.

Norms and Permission

When a person-in-charge is new to an existing functional or healthy group, the smartest thing she does is hide; in other words, she keeps a low profile while she learns about the culture. When new, the more she fits the norms for her position in terms of appearance and behaviors the better. In the following graphic, initials are used to represent norms: V—visual (appearance), A—auditory (voice patterns), K—kinesthetic (movement, body posture), B—breathing.

---

x norms of V A K B

Because she is not highly visible, she can observe and absorb the culture faster and more accurately. Once accepted in a functional or healthy culture, she lets more of her idiosyncrasies out. Think of what political cartoonists do: they exaggerate a famous person's physical feature or habit, and that exaggeration becomes a symbol of the person's uniqueness. Once the person-in-charge is seen as competent, the more different she is, the more the difference adds to her charismatic appeal. This includes being taller (according to Malcolm Gladwell,[31] the average male CEO is three inches taller than the average male) or shorter, heavier or lighter, male or female, old or young, etc. Examples abound:

- Gandhi's shirtless and glasses

- JFK's accent

- Churchill's ever-present cigar and bathtub. Taking a long bath increased his creativity. He invented the term, "The Iron Curtain" while soaking in the tub.

- The bushy eyebrows of Groucho Marx and Albert Einstein.

- The hats of Fidel Castro and Ché Gueverra

- The noses of Jimmy Durante, Danny Thomas, and Barbara Streisand

> *When we are new to a group, we try to fit in, to "hide." Yet, once accepted, what was formerly a blemish becomes our trademark.*

$$x$$

norms of V A K B

Often public figures have a "public person" which, while charismatic, may belie their "private person." John Fitzgerald Kennedy and Martin Luther King's public personas were charismatic while their private personas lacked character. The tendency is to sing the lyrics of "...Abraham, Martin and John...the good they die young." Yet, as tragic as their early deaths were, in terms of their images, it might be best that they did die young in that their human frailties (e.g., marital and health difficulties) didn't come out when they were alive.

Other famous people, such as Nelson Mandela and Gandhi, have led long, exemplary lives.

Suffice it to say, a competent person-in-charge of a functional or healthy group adds to her influence by having unique, outside-the-norms appearance, behaviors, styles, and values. In addition, if she is blessed to be a person of outstanding character, that only adds to the respect people afford her. She is a blend of both dog and cat traits, and as such, she is a liaison with positional authority. Dogs will love her because of how she reveals her *person*. Cats will admire her because of how she handles her *position*.

> *A charismatic leader has*
> *a followship of dogs and*
> *a fellowship of cats.* [32]

7-3

Permission Begets Permission

There is a phenomenon of group dynamics that the person-in-charge does well to take into account. As recommended above, when the person-in-charge is new she stays within the group norms. Once she is known and accepted, she operates outside the norms in one or more ways.

So here is the formula: If a person-in-charge is new and goes outside group norms, the person-in-charge will have less permission than she would have had if she had been inside the norms. But it changes with time. Once the person-in-charge is accepted by her group, if she stays completely within the norms she will have less permission than if she has gone outside of the norms. The important question isn't whether the person-in-charge is "in or out of the norm," but rather, When does she fit in with the norms and when does she depart from them?" The axiom is:

> *When new and unknown, blend in.*
> *When known and accepted, be different.*

This principle also applies to a person-in-charge who vulnerably reveals her person. Again, the question isn't *whether* she reveals her personal side; the important question is *when* she does. Once she is known and accepted, the person-in-charge can expose her humanness. When JFK was making an historical appearance in Berlin, he attempted to say in German, "I am a Berliner." He misspoke and said something like, "I am a jelly dough-nut." But because he had permission to be there in the first place, his attempt to be a respectful guest and speak in the language of the host nation meant that his vulnerable mistake endeared him even more to the audience.

If President George W. Bush were to make the same kind of mistake, it wouldn't work, not because of the mistake but because of his lack of permission with the German people. Just as "the rich get richer...," permission begets more permission.

This explains why a person-in-charge who has permission and displays justified anger, annoyance, or disappointment will find that it has expanded her personal influence even more.

Balance

A healthy person-in-charge balances her doglike and cat-like behaviors. She can't be too dog-oriented because when she operates solely from her heart, she will feel guilty if she thinks she is causing discomfort and pain to an individual. Meanwhile, the group is likely to experience the discomfort and pain of wasted time and a too-soft approach to accountability. Likewise, a healthy person-in-charge can't be too cat-oriented because when she operates solely from her head, she will be heartless and inhumane towards the individual. This over-emphasis on results will be equally uncomfortable to the group.

> *A healthy leader has control and balance between her heart and head.*

Dog-oriented persons-in-charge are people-oriented. Cat persons-in-charge are issue-oriented. When the person-in-charge operates solely from one style, she usually ends up managing individuals rather than the group as a whole. This does not work well if the goal is healthy group functioning. Effective group dynamics requires skill in managing for the sake of the group.

Vignette: Civil War Generals

Sometimes a look at historical figures will help us understand current times. The following Civil War story can bring increased clarity to understanding group dynamics in today's world.[33]

General George McClellan was a doglike person-in-charge. He loved his troops, so much so that he referred to them as his "sons." He couldn't commit his troops to the necessary sacrifice of a bloody battle.

General Ulysses S. Grant (who later became the President) was a catlike person-in-charge. He was more than willing to commit troops for the cause of a campaign. His nickname was "butcher."

General Robert E. Lee was a charismatic person-in-charge, a leader. He balanced the value of human life with the larger picture of war. Even his offensive engagements were orchestrated with a defensive posture. There is a story that symbolizes his relationship with his troops. The army was returning from a long day of battle, and as they crossed a bridge to the camp, the word spread that the general was asleep in a nearby tent. His men did their best to tip-toe across the bridge so as not to disturb his sleep.

Travel Tips—The Path to Charismatic Leadership

The path to charismatic leadership may seem direct, but it isn't. If you are dog-oriented, your style of being the person-in-charge is to facilitate.

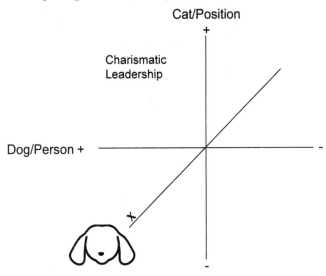

Your path to becoming more of a charismatic leader isn't direct in that you don't go straight from "dog" to "charisma."

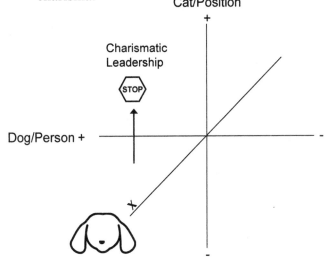

7-4

For a dog to achieve charisma, the route is traveled by first developing cat qualities.

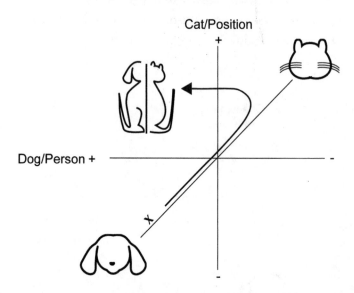

If you are cat-oriented your style of being the person-in-charge is to manage.

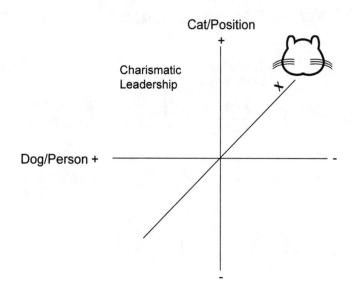

Your path to becoming more of a charismatic leader isn't direct, either.

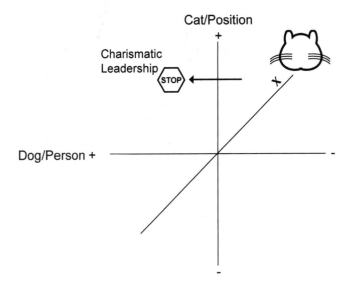

For a cat to achieve charisma, the route is traveled by first developing dog qualities.

7-5

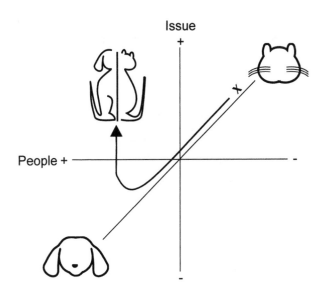

By developing both our cat and dog qualities, we avoid the trap of having to choose between one or the other. By not being confined to either cat (credible, pilot, and positional) or dog (approachable, flight attendant, personal), we end up having the whole range of behaviors.*

A charismatic leader can operate anywhere on the functional diagonal line. When things are going well, her flexibility allows her to be more dog-oriented and to put a premium on each individual. When times are tough, she is forced to be more cat-oriented. She doesn't have the luxury of an individual emphasis—the group comes first.

7-6

Charlie Chaplin

Whenever a person-in-charge expands her repertoire, there is an awkward time during the learning curve when she does not feel like she is being herself. This is especially true while the person-in-charge is learning how to select the appropriate level of being dog and cat. After doing a new habit or skill for a while, the behavior feels familiar and she adds it to how she defines herself. There is a story that brings laughter and comfort to us as we learn to increase our self-image.

Charlie Chaplin, the famous silent film actor, was vacationing at the French Riviera. He learned that the Mediterranean resort he was staying at was hosting a Charlie Chaplin look alike contest. He entered and came in third place.

---

*See *Charisma—The Art of Relationships* pp. 27-35 for details on cat and dog qualities.

> *Our self-image is the number one variable that influences our professional growth.*

Educate the Unconscious

7-7

A healthy person-in-charge is a healthy expert, someone who knows a lot. But there are different kinds of experts, and not all are healthy. A cat-oriented expert knows a lot, but the cat's pride tends to get in the way of admitting what the cat doesn't know—thus blind spots are created. She deludes herself (and others) in thinking that she knows something when she doesn't. Her lack of ease at admitting she doesn't know everything prevents her from being open and continuing to learn.

A healthy expert knows a lot, and she knows what she doesn't know. Moreover, she is comfortable not knowing—thus the healthy expert is open and comfortable as she continues to learn. Because the healthy expert has self-honesty, she knows when and when not to trust her intuition.[34] She simply has to educate her unconscious mind and then she can trust it.

She understands that you really know a culture only from the inside. If the group that she inherits is functional-to-healthy, she hides for as long as she can. She trains herself to distrust any of her initial reactions and first impressions until she has been in the culture long enough to experience the nuances.

This helps her avoid the pitfall of making cross-cultural extrapolations (over-generalizations)—a faulty process. Cross-cultural generalization happens when someone who is new to a culture perceives something and interprets what it means through the filter of a previous culture, "Gee, when that happened in my previous culture, it meant ...".

As the skilled person-in-charge continues to observe her new culture, impressions start to emerge. She looks for correlations to verify those impressions. Instead of operating from arrogance, she trains herself to be humble and to look for exceptions to her impressions. She is a true group anthropologist.

When does the person-in-charge trust her gut? She can trust her instincts when she can breathe well, because it means that she is comfortable; she knows she can trust herself when she feels no anxiety over a course of action. On the other hand, when she is sleep deprived, angry, or emotionally stressed, she will breathe high and thereby have a reminder that in this situation, she can't trust her instincts.

Dr. Gerard Hodgkinson, a professor at Leeds University Business School, says there are times when it is important to follow any impulses that accompany high breathing, such as when someone fears for their safety.[35]

As a person-in-charge, she knows that the threat of physical danger is a valid exception to the rule that says, "Trust abdominal breathing; distrust high breathing." When anyone feels physically unsafe or threatened, the high breathing releases chemicals of fight or flight, so when your safety is involved, trust your gut.

Peer Relationships

Functional groups are based on the person-in-charge's relationship with the group. Healthy groups are based on the relationship the members have with one other.

Vignette: Great Servers

Sean is someone I greatly admire as a restaurant server. He worked for the most prestigious chain in our big city of Portland, Oregon. On those occasions when our family has had dinner there, his precise attention to detail was amazing.

Once he said, "Michael, you teach people to have a range of behaviors and the wisdom to know when to use which behavior. You teach 'pattern recognition.' The good servers work hard. Using your terminology, the good dog servers are trying to please everyone: the clients, the chefs, and their fellow servers. Their signature is a perpetual smile. The good cat servers individually decide what is important to them and act accordingly. If it is to get the food to the customers, then they tend to bully their co-workers so that they get their dishes immediately.

"The great servers walk fast in the kitchen and slower around the patrons who are enjoying their meal. They will be very civil and cooperative around everyone, but when they see behavior by an employee that could be detrimental to the establishment, they either deal directly with the person or they report the incident to the manager. Also, they can separate what is happening in their private life from their professional world.

"But 'relationship' is the biggest secret! The good server establishes rapport with each customer at the table. When the customer enjoys the server's care, the tip will be greater. The great server does even more in that she establishes rapport amongst the customers because customers spend more time with one another than with the server. When diners have a good time with each other, the server's tip is even greater.

Preference is to Operate from Person

The charismatic leader's first preference is to operate from her person, and yet she is comfortable with operating from her position.

Vignette: First His Person, then His Position

Marcus drove from the airport to the district office reflecting on how in seven years with the company, he had climbed to the rank of regional manager. He chuckled to himself as he thought of all the good and bad bosses he had had. The good ones were models for him. At the same time, he would not have fully appreciated why the effective bosses were effective if he had not witnessed the effect of bad bosses.

As soon as he parked his car at the district office, he instinctively grabbed his clipboard and started to open the car door. Then he caught himself, took a deep breath, and relaxed. He had almost made the mistake of walking into the office with the symbol of his position—the clipboard. One of the lessons he had learned the hard way was to first make contact with the satellite office workers as a "person." After shaking hands with everyone and accepting a cup of coffee he returned to the rental car. This time he walked into the office holding the clipboard. Now it was time for business.

Systematically Inconsistent

The person-in-charge of a functional dog group is consistent. The person-in-charge of a functional cat group is also consistent. In both cases, she operates from a set of rules and protocols. The set of rules and protocols that work for one group may not work for another group. When the appropriate rules and protocols are adhered to, the subordinates feel safe because they know what to expect.

The person-in-charge of a dysfunctional group is usually inconsistent. The group does not know what to expect.

The person-in-charge of a healthy group is also inconsistent. However, the group does know what to expect. The leader has a set of principles from which she operates. The leader of a healthy group is flexible. If the situation is easy, the person-in-charge emphasizes the individual corner. When the situation is difficult, the person-in-charge emphasizes the group corner.

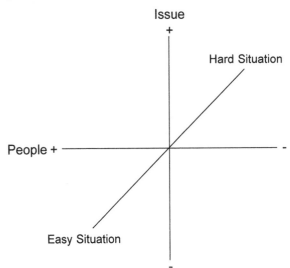

7-8

Taking Care of Herself
Reviewing the day in third person

While the person-in-charge would rather not make mistakes, she accepts that she will make them, and she has a three-step review strategy for accelerated growth.

1. She avoids guilt by reviewing a difficult day in third person. Instead of saying to herself, "I really blew it when 'x' happened…" she substitutes either her gender pronoun ("she" "he") or her title ("chairperson" "CEO" department head"): "She really blew it when 'x' happened…".

2. She does a gigantic laugh at herself. She knows if she can't laugh, she can't learn. She needs oxygen to the brain to successfully process what happened and to create alternative options. If she can't laugh about 'x' and the 'x' is likely to happen then she seeks professional assistance.

3. With her brain refreshed by oxygen from the laughter, she then begins the process of developing alternative options. She now switches to first person. She knows she is really doing well when she can rehearse a future scenario as if she were Walt Disney creating an exaggerated cartoon version of future success.* She says sentences that start off with, "What I plan to do is…." "The next time I find myself in a similar situation I will …."

> *Review in third person. Program in first person.*

———

*If she is spiritual, this is where she asks for and accepts God's grace.

Breathing

The section that follows refers to high and shadow breathing vs. low and abdominal breathing. For a full explanation, including the importance of emphasizing exhalation, see pages 113-134 of *The Elusive Obvious*.

A healthy expert uses the concept "Breathing Abdominally = Trust ('BAT')" as a measure of how well she can trust her gut. Even if she is part of a culture she knows very well, if the decision she needs to make is quite important she does BAT. She places one hand on her abdomen and the other hand on her opposite shoulder. She knows that if the hand on the abdomen goes in and out when she is thinking about the upcoming situation, she is breathing low—she can trust her gut. If the hand on the shoulder moves as she is thinking about the upcoming situation, she is breathing high—she either can't trust, or will trust her gut less.

She uses BAT not only on herself but with others. When she receives an oral report or recommendation she judges the other person's congruence based on his BAT. If he breathes low/abdominal when reporting or suggesting, she adds more weight to the accuracy of the information. If the person breathes high/shallow, she questions if he is certain about what he is saying. She uses BAT as a quick physiological way to assess a person's congruency.

The Person-in-charge's Seasonal Energy

7-9

There are three kinds of jobs: working with people, ideas, and things (for example, tools). Usually, the most stressful of the three is working with people, which is what a person-in-charge does day after day. As the seasons become long, specifically when the calendar is between vacations, fatigue starts to set in. This is when productivity decreases and mistakes increase. Seasonally, the person-in-charge has to monitor her own energy level.

She also monitors others' energy level. Dr. Bill Sommers, who mentors system administrators' professional development, has an axiom, "If we don't feed our middle managers, they will eat our front-line employees."

As previously mentioned, a person-in-charge's comfort is verified with her BAT. Simply put, if the person-in-charge is in stress (high/shallow breathing) while doing an authoritarian interaction or, more importantly, immediately following the exchange, it's an indication that the person-in-charge isn't comfortable with herself. By staying fit, she will breathe better during challenging interactions, and she will find she is more energetic and effective.

Travel Tips—Fitness

When our schedule starts getting crowded, we tend to neglect our own fitness. Being fit helps us dissociate from volatile situations and maintain an external focus as we "stay outside ourselves." We find it easier to focus on how the group is doing. We think instead of feel.

The irony is that we tend to have the same seasonal energy as our subordinates. When a product, protocol or project is about to launch, the excitement is contagious. We don't need to be fit then. But towards the end of the campaign, everyone is low on energy, including us. As we seasonally get rundown, we withdraw from being outside ourselves and instead pay attention to our own thoughts and emotions. We don't notice group dynamic developments. We become re-active, and in so doing, we are less competent and more often surprised.

Have a different season than subordinates. By staying fit, especially when others are not, we weather their season.

Associated vs. Dissociated[36]

7-10

While exercising is the best medicine for weathering the doldrums of the season, there are other coping behaviors which increase the person-in-charge's ability to stay outside herself. The more she slouches, the more she goes inside; by contrast, the more she is upright in body position the more she can stay outside herself. It is no small coincidence that visual-oriented persons-in-charge, famous for a posture that their grandmothers would be proud of, are less in touch with themselves. And kinesthetic-oriented persons-in-charge, with a tendency to slouching, are more associated and aware of bodily or emotional discomforts. There is also a correlation between the person's rank in an organization: the lower the level in the organization, the more associated the person-in-charge can be and still be effective. On the higher levels, the person-in-charge needs to be dissociated to be effective.

The more one is associated, the more the person is aware of how she feels. This encompasses how well she is doing in terms of sleep, food, security, and need for privacy. "Dissociated" is a description of the state in which a person is not in touch with visceral inputs. Missing meals, fatigue, and emotional concerns do not bother the person-in-charge as much as they would if she were associated. In reality, no one is completely associated or dissociated. It is more accurate to talk about the degree of be-ing associated and dissociated than to speak as if it is a switch activating one or the other condition. That being said, every person-in-charge desires to be in voluntary control of her degree of association and dissociation.

> *In general, the more difficult the situation, the more the person-in-charge increases her degree of dissociation. Likewise, the more pleasant the moment, the more the enjoyment is experienced if she is associated.*

Throughout a season the person-in-charge will experience varying levels of fatigue. Since fatigue is usually a cumu-lative result, it is possible to predict when she is likely to be most fatigued. It is during the seasonal fatigue times that the person-in-charge is prone to feel sorry for her-self.[37] In general, the person-in-charge can expect a sea-sonal decrease in energy the longer it has been since her last vacation. She experiences a rejuvenation following vacations.

7-11

Contracts with Our Body

In addition to standing up straight so she stay outside her-self, the person-in-charge also has the option of making a contract with her body.

Here is how the contract between the mind and body works. The mind is meaning-driven. When the mind finds a task meaningful, the mind demands that the body pro-vide energy. The body will accommodate and do what the mind requests as long as the body has other periods of time when it can recharge its batteries. But sometimes the body needs to rest to replenish itself and the mind is still demanding "full steam ahead!" The mind is so associated with the "meaningful experience" that it has become dissociated from its body.

This is when the body does a silent or loud protest and closes down. This is a physiological version of the cycle of Accommodate, Accommodate, Explode (page 128) Literally, the body tells the mind, "I know you have found this experience very meaningful and without your knowing it, I have become exhausted. I am closing us down for repair!"

The person-in-charge can make a contract with the body, "Please give me the time and energy to concentrate and focus, and I promise that I will make sure we have rest and downtime when…." This contract is like an emotional weekend ATM: we are withdrawing energy that isn't actually in the bank. This analogy is a practical way of explaining why it is critical that we keep our contract. If we keep our promise to ourselves that we will rest and recharge our batteries, the body trusts the mind and will be willing to agree to the next time the mind wants a contract. But it we don't keep our promise, the bank of energy remembers and won't lend us energy the next time the mind tries to negotiate a contract. We have to put the money in the bank before it opens on Monday.

7-12

A Healthy Group Defined

In some ways this chapter and the next are the reason Inside Track was written. All chapters lead to "Healthy Groups." Here is a graphic view of this journey and a summary of how a healthy group is a blend of dog and cat traits.

The Issue—People axis offers a visual graphic of where a healthy group fits in comparison with groups in previous chapters.

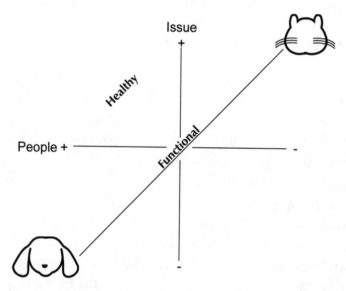

When a functional group moves away from the center, becoming either too dog-oriented or too cat-oriented, it gets unbalanced and tends to become dysfunctional.

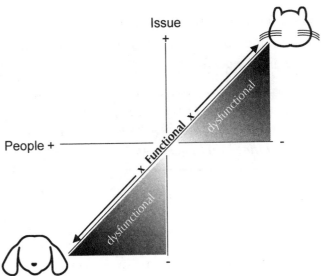

An extreme dog-oriented culture emphasizes the individual and acceptance of the individual, even if this is to the detriment of the group as a whole. An extreme cat-oriented culture emphasizes the group and accountability, even if it leads in the destruction of individuals.

By contrast, a healthy group is often a result of a functional group moving towards the center. A healthy group has a balance of dog and cat traits.

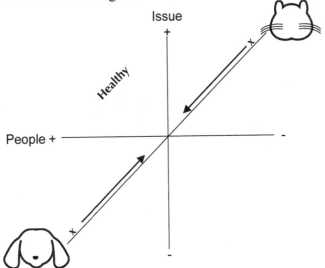

Once a functional group is a blend of dog and cat traits, transforming a functional group into a healthy group calls for the art of leadership.

> *A healthy group is one in which the individual is accepted as a person and the individual is held accountable for her behavior.*

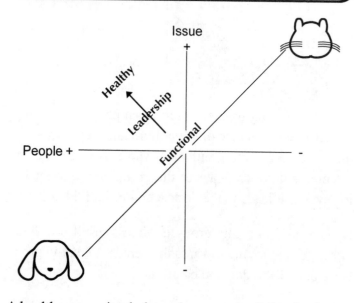

A healthy group is a balance between the following opposites:

Dog	Cat
Person	Position
Acceptance	Accountability
Morale	Productivity
Influence	Power
Pride	Ambition
Support	Challenge

In the chart on the next page, the first item in each group is a dog trait and the second item is a cat trait. Each pair of traits is followed by a description of the blend of that set of dog and cat traits.

Management—The Key to a Healthy Group

A healthy group has a balance of dog and cat traits: the individual is accepted as a person and the individual is held accountable for his behavior. Usually a group is healthy because of the leadership of the person-in-charge.

DOG TRAIT	CAT TRAIT
People can be accommodating	and ambitiously willing to risk.
Person: People can be themselves	*Position:* and can get their job done.
Acceptance: Regard for people coexists	*Accountability:* with high expectation for competence.
Morale: People are acknowledged for contributions	*Productivity:* but slackers are not tolerated.
Influence: Operations based on relationships is the norm	*Power:* yet power is used when needed.
Pride: The culture supports continuous improvement	*Ambition:* and allows failure during the learning curve
Support: Structure provides resources	*Challenging:* and rewards for experimental work.

Skillful and artistic management is key to a healthy culture. Any person-in-charge can be the head of a group when things are going swimmingly. But eventually people have to be managed. How the person-in-charge manages will greatly affect the group's health. A leader operates from these four concepts:

1. Manage the Behavior, Not the Person.

2. Move from Stereotypes to Full Humans.

3. Share Leadership.

4. Confirm the Group's Sanity.

7-13

1. Manage the Behavior, Not the Person

How does the person-in-charge manage an inappropriate individual's *behavior* and still keep that person's self-image as a person intact? The answer is found in not making eye contact during management.

Two-point vs. Three-point Communication

Eye contact is referred to as two-point communication because there are two parties involved in the communication: the person-in-charge and the individual. Two-point communication is interpersonal; it accesses the relationship and it heightens the emotions between the parties. Use two-point communication when the interaction is positive.

If the person-in-charge looks at the agenda, the individual will follow her eyes and look at the agenda also. Since the two parties, namely the person-in-charge and the individual, are now looking at a third point, the communication is referred to as a three-point communication. Three-point communication is more impersonal, and by focusing on the issues represented on the visual third point, the interaction becomes less emotional for both parties.[38] Use three-point communication when the interaction is negative.

When managing, once the person-in-charge has the individual's attention, if she looks solely at the third point and doesn't look at the individual, the unconscious interpretation is that the person-in-charge is only managing the individual's behavior. If you want to be more comfortable in your own catness, get in the habit of using a third point. The exception is big cats. Big cats will want us to look them in the eye and, without blinking, "give it to them straight."[39]

2. Move Stereotypes to Full Humans

7-14

So far, this work has defined a healthy group as one in which the individual is managed with respect. This involves the "person-in-charge" corner interacting with the "individual" corner of the group triangle.

Of equal importance, but of a more difficult nature, is the interaction between the "group" corner and the "individual" corner. It is an innate tendency of group dynamics for a group to gravitate towards stereotyping the individual members of the group.

Chapter Two introduced the idea that outliers within the group can be defined as "people the group notices and pays attention to." The person-in-charge may or may not see these people as outliers, but her opinion doesn't matter; she needs to take them into account simply because of the attention the group gives these "noticed" individuals. Chapter Two mentioned the fact that outliers are different from the rest of the group—they are noticed.

Stereotyping provides people with a sense of how individuals and the group as a whole will act. However false this is, it still provides a sense of identity for individuals and the grup. The criteria used for the stereotyping tends to change over time. Listed below are five phases of stereotyping.

Stereotyping cannot be prevented. The question is how to utilize this innate tendency. The faster the group is formed, the more the criteria used for stereotyping changes from external appearances and behaviors to internal traits, values and character.

I. External Physical Differences

When a group is unformed, people notice members who are unique—the outliers. Since people only have first impression, they notice members who are physically different. Anyone who is taller, smaller, thinner or heavier than others is noticed. Anyone who wears different clothing, has different skin color and facial features is noticed.

HEIGHT	WEIGHT	CLOTHING	SKIN COLOR	FACIAL FEATURES
*				
Norm	Norm	Norm	Norm	Norm

II. External Behavioral Differences

As the members are around each other more, they start to notice differences in behaviors. Anyone who is different in terms of rapid movement, loud talk, longer talking, big gestures and punctuality is noticed.

―――

*A "ladder" is the vertical equivalent of the horizontal graphic on page 46.

MOVES	TALKS	GESTURES
Fast	Loud	A Lot
Slow	Soft	A Little

III. Internal Traits Differences

As the members become formed and functioning with each other, they notice internal differences. Mental and emotional traits, styles of thinking and listening are noticed. A "halo" or generalizing process occurs. An individual who is ranked high on certain positive traits is assumed to also have other positive traits. This is stereotyping of correlations. The same process occurs with individuals who rank low on certain traits. They will be seen as being ranked low on other traits.

SMART	THINKS	CONTRIBUTES
Most	Quickly	Much
Least	Slowly	Little

IV. Cultural Values

As the group becomes healthy, certain values are given greater significance. Members tend to rank each other based on the degree that individuals exhibit those values. Some cultures emphasize *personal* values such as integrity, sincerity, genuineness, authenticity and ability to form personal relationships. Some cultures focus more on *positional* values such as productivity, efficiency, effectiveness and ability to form working relationships.

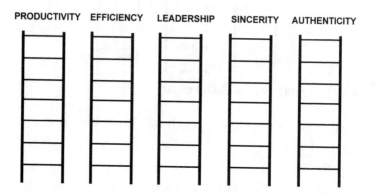

V. Internal Character Differences

If a crisis occurs, the character becomes known and ranked.

 Travel Tips—Political Correctness

The western world has been engulfed in a wave of political correctness. Stereotyping based on appearance is a "no-no." Yet from a group dynamic standpoint, appearance is the only criterion that distinguishes people in an unformed group.

If you are like me, we are committed above all to humane communication and respectful treatment of our fellow human beings and, at the same time, we are committed to understanding group dynamics. The faster a group is formed and becomes functional and healthy, the faster the criteria of stereotyping progress from appearances to behaviors to mental styles to core values.

> *Reshaping stereotyping allows the participant to blossom into a fuller person.*

On the surface it would seem that the individual would accept the stereotypical image if the identity is positive, such as "best looking," "very smart" and "fastest worker." But a closer look will show that this is not necessarily true; it seems that acceptance of the identity is based not on whether the image is negative or positive but on whether the identity is voluntarily accepted. If the individual wants the identity, whether it is positive or negative, she will welcome the role. When the identity is imposed on the individual, she may well resent the imposition.

Why does stereotyping continue to exist? Each corner of the group dynamics triangle is vested in maintaining the stereotypes. The individual is interested in maintaining the image because it gives him an identity, and a person would rather have some identity than no identity. This also explains why a worker will continue to act in an inappropriate manner: such behavior provides the security of a given identity. This also explains why the majority of people who are abused at home and are counseled towards a different living arrangement will tend to resist. The other two corners are drawn to stereotyping, too. Why? Because it helps them know what to expect from different members of the group. To most people, the familiar is more comfortable than the new or the unknown.

> *Most people are more comfortable with the familiar than with the new or unknown.*

7-15~16

Scapegoat

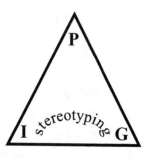

Groups naturally gravitate towards a pecking order. The most destructive result of a pecking order is that it creates a scapegoat. Found at the bottom of the pecking order, the scapegoat is a person or subgroup who is seen by the rest of the group as the cause of problems. This hierarchical order is represented by the ladder, and the individual at the bottom is on the lowest rung of the group dynamics ladder.

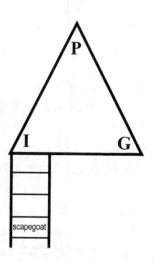

The ladder effect is especially present when inappropriate behavior appears. The person at the bottom rung of the ladder becomes the "whipping boy."[40] In time, all the group members expect inappropriate behavior from the individual. Often the dynamics include the person-in-charge over-managing the individual, sometimes subtly but blatantly at other times. This includes comments like, "Well, we all know that Joe is always late!" In certain groups the same individual is at the bottom of the ladder regardless of whether it is the punctuality ladder, the productivity ladder, or the good listener ladder. Other groups have different ladders for different behaviors, so that a person who is never punctual might not be the same individual who is always fiddling around instead of listening (for example, "Sally, PLEASE LISTEN!!").

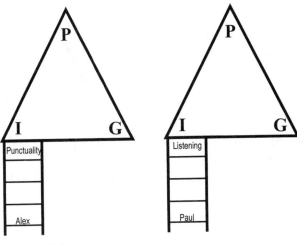

Because of the security of a given identity, the individual often clings to a set of behaviors. The other two corners of the group triangle are also interested in maintaining the stereotypes because of predictability. From a management perspective, both the person-in-charge and the group know—and

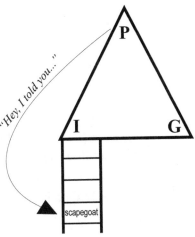

are comforted by knowing—who will and won't need to be managed. For example, if several workers are acting inappropriately and the scapegoat is one of them, it is likely the person-in-charge will reprimand the scapegoat.

When the person-in-charge, however inadvertently she might be doing so, reprimands one or two workers more often than is actually warranted, scapegoats are created. Unusual as it might be, if the group is starting to be inappropriate and instead of reprimanding the scapegoat, the person-in-charge calls on a worker who is perceived as liked by the person-in-charge, then the group clearly gets it that the person-in-charge is displeased with the behavior and not the person. This form of sorting whom to manage

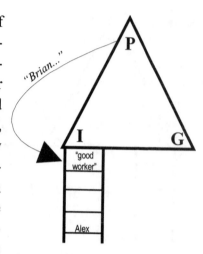

whenever a group of people are behaving inappropriately will assist the group in understanding that the purpose of the business place is productivity. Thus management can be done quickly, amnesia occurs, and the group can get back to work.

For a healthy group, it is imperative that the person-in-charge find something that she genuinely likes about the individual that she will eventually manage. This breaks the cycle of the managed individual feeling disliked, as in "You always pick on me."

While the individual corner may find it wonderful that the person-in-charge likes him, it is even more important that the group perceive that the person-in-charge likes the individual that she might have to manage. Why? In the above example the per-

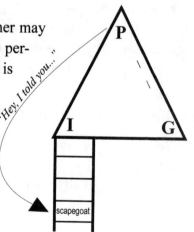

son-in-charge could afford to wait until a "good" worker joined the misbehaving group. As previously mentioned, when the person-in-charge manages a "good" worker, the group knows she is displeased with the behavior. However, there will be more occasions when she cannot afford to wait for the "good" worker to join in; most of the time, the person-in-charge does not have the luxury of waiting for a "star employee" to momentarily misbehave.

> *The person-in-charge needs to be perceived as liking all employees, especially those she is most likely to manage.*

The question arises, "Why is management of the "good" worker such an uncommon practice?" The answer is found in the opposite direction, "What is the benefit of managing only the scapegoat?" Except for the scapegoat, the members who are misbehaving improve their behavior and the relationship between the person-in-charge and these individuals is preserved. In the true sense of the word, the scapegoat isn't a goat at all but more like a sacrificial lamb, delivered up for the good of the person-in-charge's relationship with the rest of the group.

How can a person-in-charge find out if her own behavior is inadvertently reinforcing the scapegoat's inappropriate behavior? Let's examine two groups: person-in-charge A and person-in-charge B both have scapegoats in their groups.

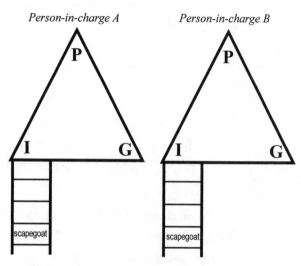

If the pattern is, when a scapegoat is removed, no new scapegoat appears in A's group, then A is a healthy person-in-charge. If the pattern is, when a scapegoat is removed, another scapegoat appears in B's group, then B is less than a healthy person-in-charge. Most people in charge of others claim that it is the workers who determine the success and ease of the group interactions. Which is true. But it is also true, that success comes from the person-in-charge's behavioral and emotional imprint on the group.

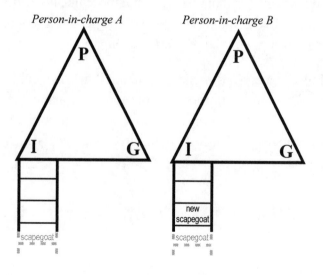

Reshape Stereotyping

A person-in-charge can't entirely prevent stereotyping. The question is, how does she reshape the group dynamics to make a positive use of the natural tendency to create stereotypes? She does it by fostering a culture in which "anyone can become as skilled as anyone else." This section provides the reshaping tools that will help her develop this healthy culture.

The goal of healthy group management is to recognize our cultural tendency to generalize from an individual's behavior to the individual as a person. This tendency is true apart from whether the individual exhibits negative or positive behaviors. If the high productivity worker makes a mistake, the worker is still a good person. And, equally true, if an at-risk (at-risk of being dysfunctional and disruptive) worker behaves well or produces outstanding work, in no way does the individual's value as a human being increase. In a healthy culture, the value of an individual person is absolute and unrelated to their value as a worker in the group.

> *In a healthy culture, the value of an individual person is absolute and unrelated to their value as a worker in the group.*

From a group dynamics vantage point, a positive identity assigned to the individual can be as emotionally isolating as any negative identity. And, even more important, the existence of stereotypes deprives each person of seeing himself as a complex human with a full range of assets and liabilities.

The definition of a healthy group is one in which each individual is accepted as a person and, at the same time, each individual is held accountable for his behavior. "Accepted as a person" involves the creating of an environment where a person's many facets are encouraged. In contrast, stereotyping is a one-dimensional group dynamic process whereby members of a group are seen in predictable images. Predictable images allow everyone to be comfortable; the person-in-charge can count on certain people to act in certain ways. Likewise, the group is able to know what roles and functions will be done by which members and, lastly, the individual person has an identity. In essence, the person's behavior and the *person* have been generalized together. As people-in-charge, we have the tendency to say, "Well, we all know Sally is smart." "Fred is such a clown."

> *A healthy group is one where the individual is known apart from his behaviors.*

In literature the main characters are described as "round" and the minor members of the story as "flat." Stereotyping results in flat human beings. The reader learns the many complexities of the major character while the minor character is assigned just one or more simple traits to support the plot. So too, in the group, the more facets each individual shows in the group, the healthier the individual and the healthier the group atmosphere.

The person-in-charge acknowledges the abilities and attributes that each member of the group displays. And, at the same time, she fosters each individual to be even more than he sees himself as being.

Standard-bearers Foster Full Humans

7-17

The person-in-charge reshapes stereotyping in her group so that individuals become full human beings. The early formation of stereotypes is the grist for her mill as she fosters full humans.

Correlations

As group formation occurs, the uniqueness of each individual begins to emerge. Statistically speaking, the people who are noticed first are usually identified with one characteristic. If an individual is seen as having more than one characteristic, then the traits tend to be correlated; for example, the highly productive worker is "serious." Often different ladders (for example, humorous) reverse the pecking order.

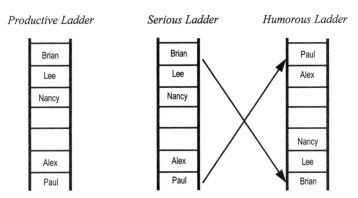

During the initial stages of stereotyping, certain workers surface as standard-bearers of different traits. The noticeable standard-bearers, such as "the group clown" and "the brain," unconsciously mold the workers into thinking that "each person finds his niche in life." These standard-bearers are critical in achieving one of the goals of a healthy group—fostering full human beings. How? Since the standard-bearers are the salient models of what human beings are, if they themselves manifest a full range of traits, then the rest of the workers believe that it is normal for one's personality to include a full range of behaviors. The goal is for the person-in-charge to elicit humor from the highly productive worker and to elicit seriousness from the group clown. In the area of management, if there is a person labeled by the group as a "problem worker," the level of healthiness that the group can arrive at is limited.

7-18

Sandwich

If workers are both praised and reprimanded in clusters and the clusters are cross-stereotyped, health is increased. If Brian Brain is singled out ("I appreciated Brian's suggestion"), then the group unconsciously thinks, "Sure, Brian can achieve such heights because he is 'the brain.'"

If Brian's name is mentioned with two other "smart" workers (Lee and Nancy), then the group is fostering hierarchy.

On the other hand, if Brian's name is mentioned with two of the group clowns, then everyone can be anyone. "When you get some spare time look at the theme that Paul, Brian, and Alex created for our holiday party."

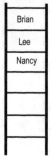

Brain Ladder

Brian
Lee
Nancy

The term sandwich is used because the person who doesn't typically belong in the category of individual being mentioned is placed in the middle of the individuals who, from a stereotypical standpoint, do belong there. In the previous example, it was clown-brain-clown. The unspoken but powerful implication was the even clowns can be smart, and even smart people can have a sense of humor.

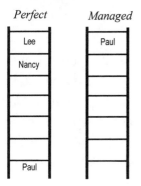

In the management arena, by sandwiching the "scapegoat" with people who are seen as behaving appropriately, the caste system is broken. The person-in-charge says, "The discussion with Brain Brian, Problem Paul and Linear Lee has produced some interesting concepts...."

Vignette: Michelangelo and the Sistine Chapel

The following is a supposedly true and humorous example of sandwiching a "good" person among the "bad."

When Michelangelo was painting the Sistine Chapel, a particular Cardinal kept intervening. The nosy official would visit the work in progress and criticize Michelangelo's work. The Cardinal would also ask the Pope to order Michelangelo to make changes. The artist finally put his foot down and prevented the Cardinal from entering the building. When the chapel was finished there was an opening ceremony. Much to the Cardinal's chagrin, he found a facsimile of his face sand-

> wiched between the faces of the damned souls
> in the portion of the painting depicting hell.

7-19

Healthy Humor

Laughing is one of the fastest ways to get a group to breathe. When the humor is done so that laughter occurs in unison, instant health is gained momentarily. But humor is often done at the expense of a person or subgroup. Someone once said that adult comedians would be lost for material if sex and drinking were off limits. As Charles Schulz says, "Strangely enough, pleasant things are not really funny. You cannot create humor out of happiness."[41]

Everyone has experienced healthy humor. But what is it? It would be easy to say, "Healthy group humor happens when laughter is not at the expense of an individual or subgroup." But greater clarity is called for. If all three corners perceive that the humor stems from the individual's behavior and not the individual as a person, then it is healthy humor. This kind of humor is liberating because the individual can laugh and the group can identify with the same behavior.

> *Healthy humor is when the group laughs "with the individual" instead of "at the individual."*

7-20

Leaders, Barometers and Liaisons Over Time

Stereotyping is common in functional groups. The membership in subgroups remains the same and the leaders and barometers stay the same. Predictability is high.

A functional group moves towards becoming healthy when the leadership for a project, protocol, or product development is based on the skills needed. Different members lead based on qualities needed for the particular task. There is a pool of talent.

In a healthy group, there is more sharing of leadership.[42] When leadership is shared, it is sometimes difficult to tell who the leader is because leading is done by a subgroup or by the group as a whole. A small group might lead the launching of a project, protocol, or product. Members belong to so many subgroups that "opposing camps" are non-existent.

> *The greater the flux among members, the healthier the system.*

One of the indicators that the dynamics of leadership in a healthy group can change as conditions change is that there is a blending of who does what; the words *always* and *never* (e.g., "Sally always gets assigned to the interesting projects." "I never get to head a committee.") are markedly absent. The ad hoc "committee" is a popular and effective way of getting things done in the group.

The healthier the group, the more workers' full personalities come out. This means that there are many subgroups, and each individual belongs to several subgroups. The importance of certain subgroups can change. For example, when a new manager is assigned, initially the subgroup of skeptics ("Let's check out the new person-in-charge.") might be influential but in time the skeptics' influence fades.

7-21

Liaison

Any discussion of leaders and a healthy group must include the concept of liaison. This individual floats between several subgroups. A liaison is an individual seen by some of his peers as being credible-oriented; they see him as someone who values productivity and considers the group to be more important than the individuals. But this same person is perceived by other colleagues as being approachable-oriented; they see him as someone who is committed to high morale and relationships with individual members of the group.

> *"Life's a dance you learn as you go. Sometimes you lead, sometimes you follow."*[43]

A liaison's flexibility is such that sometimes he is a "lead" and other times a "support." The varied ways in which this individual is viewed by her co-workers indicate that the liaison is not stuck in a given mold. The liaison shatters the confines of stereotyping. In essence, liaisons supercede and therefore replace the concept of leaders and barometers.

Because of the person-in-charge's development of shared leadership, the group is healthier. Techniques to broaden the base of leadership are:

- Have individuals belong to many subgroups so they will be seen as having many facets (page 52).

- Foster members who are not noticed into being noticed (page 53, Fostered Leaders).

- Have Standard Bearers broaden their range of behaviors; especially look for opportunities to shatter Correlations (page 177).

- Have liaisons replace or supplement positional leadership (page 180).

- Defer to expertise amongst the members (page 186, Levels of Leadership).

The liaison in a healthy group sets a positive tone that permeates the group; the culture is one of getting things done while being respectful of people involved. How specifically does the liaison contribute to the healthiness of the culture? Since he doesn't have any positional authority to demand that things get done, he must become a master at getting things done through influence. A liaison influences by understanding and working in sync with the group dynamics; usually, he will also understand the system dynamics.

> *A liaison has a unique blend of low ego,*
> *a high need to move things, and*
> *a commitment to at all times be respectful of people.*

A positional powered person is tempted by the question, "What can/shall I do?"—reflection of ego. In contrast, the liaison asks, "Who would have permission to do what needs to be done?" He understands permission as "the ability to get people to be receptive."

> *Compared to an average group,*
> *a healthy group has more liaisons.*

Travel Tips—Liaisons are Not Promoted

Liaisons are essential to move a functional group into being a healthy group. If we are members of a functional group, we can help the group progress towards being healthy by acting as liaisons between subgroups. If we are the person-in-charge, we recognize we can't do it alone—we need liaisons. If we don't have liaisons within the group, we can either foster them or hire them.

If we are a liaison, we practice the full range of dog and cat behaviors. We have flexibility and purpose. We focus on process more than outcome. We are not possessive about a given issue, but we insist that the process by which our group handles the issue be effective and respectful. Was the appropriate input gathered? Were the individuals and subgroups acknowledged? Were realistic tasks assigned and was support given to the implementation phase? As liaisons, we are the invisible lubricant that oils the human machinery.

And we may want to remain at the liaison role level. We don't have to be the parent to find great satisfaction in influencing the growth of a child. We can be an effective nanny without aspiring to be a parent.

However, if we do aspire to be promoted, there is one gigantic caution: liaisons don't usually get promoted. Why not?

It's because, as stated above, we are "invisible." We are not consciously noticed, or if we are noticed, no one wants to create the hole that would be left in the group if we were promoted. There is a strategy, though, that we liaisons can use if we seek promotions, and it's this: we have to become issue-oriented. Adopting the definitive style of a calm cat, we state our stand on issues. We offer specific suggestions. We make recommendations that are well researched and we state them in the acceptable culture style of people in higher positions of the organization.

There is another option! As effective liaisons, instead of seeking promotions inside the organization, we have the option of becoming an outside process-oriented consultant. We remain invaluable, we are very well paid, and we continue to grow professionally.

Because most functional groups tend to lack liaisons, effective outside consultants are of premium value. Groups—and even more importantly, systems—need someone who can:

- Be a go-between for opposing camps. As an objective ambassador, we can explain the other subgroup's perspective so that all members remember that they are part of the larger group.

- Take information to superiors without getting shot as the messenger. We make sure that invisible elephants are addressed.

- Facilitate and mediate as a trusted person. We are non-possessive about the specific outcome, yet completely dedicated to a fair and effective process.

- Tell the truth in a comfortable manner.

Many of these functions are outlined in Chapter Eight in the section on Power, Information, and Time Patterns (page 216).

7-22

3. Share Leadership

For unformed and short-term groups, it is appropriate for the person-in-charge to be a to have the group depend on her. Even with functional groups, the person-in-charge initially wants the leaders of subgroups to depend on her. After the group becomes formed and functioning and starts to move towards healthy she transitions the dependence on her to the members have a dependence on each other. How does she do this?

Subgroups have leaders. The members of subgroups depend on their leader; the members both look up to their leaders and anticipate that their leaders will represent the subgroup's interest. By having the leaders depend on the person-in-charge, she creates a dependence with all members. She uses her rapport with leaders of subgroups to connect those leaders to one another. If the leaders are connected the leaders' subgroup members are connect.. The following examples show a range of methods for joining leaders together.[44]

> "If you get a chance, you may want to talk with Janet and Hank about how they are individually applying some of our ideas."

> "*By* talking to Jane and Hank, you can get some new ideas on…".

> "Jane and Hank, see each other and swap your responses to some of the difficult situations we have been discussing."

> "Paul and Lee, talk to Jim and Hazel. You will likely find options to some of the difficult situations we have been discussing."

Another form of shared leadership is deferring to others.

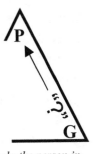

The group asks the person-in-charge a question.

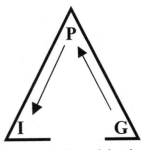

The person-in-charge defers the question to an individual,

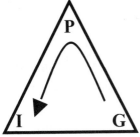

resulting in the group noticing the individual.

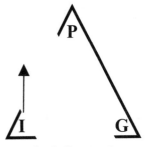

The individual's status increases.

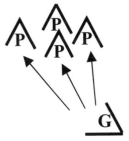

Over time the group recognizes many experts and the group is self reliant

> ***Functional groups are based on the person-in-charge's relationship with the group. Healthy groups are based members' relationships with one other.***

7-23

4. Confirm the Group's Sanity

A repeating theme of *Fast Track* is that when managing or disciplining an inappropriate individual, the person-in-charge's primary responsibility is the group's welfare. And yet, a leader accepts the fact that she can neither change nor control people or groups. She realizes that a group forms their own identity as summarized by the expression, "It is never my group, it is the group's group." If you think you can control an individual or a group, just live with teenagers for a week. If the leader can't change the individual, at least she can confirm the sanity of the group by sharing that she sees the individual the same as the group does. Confirming a group's sanity and then teaching them to ignore inappropriate behavior is critical for the group's functioning because any time an inappropriate individual succeeds in getting attention over time, it is a sign that the group is dysfunctional. A healthy group learns to ignore the individual who is consistently inappropriate.

7-24

Protecting an Individual

A leader knows that a group will have difficulty being healthy if even one member is an outcast. If the person-in-charge has the group's respect, she intervenes and indicates non-verbally that this individual is off limits to group feedback. She would do this with an individual who has inappropriate behaviors and is unable to learn from the group's criticism. Group members know that she gives some individuals more slack and latitude, and they trust that she has valid reasons for individualizing expectations.

Vignette: Autism

HR phoned Chanél. They had just interviewed a candidate, Shirley, who was cognitively qualified but had Asperger's Syndrome, a high functioning form of autism. HR wanted to know if Chanél thought her group could function with Shirley. Chanél said that she would get back with HR within 24 hours.

The next morning Chanél called an impromptu meeting. As the ten members filed into the conference room, they saw the LCD projector. Their curiosity grew as they saw Chanél wearing a knowing half-smile. "Good morning. As you know, our company has made a concerted effort to be socially responsible. HR has a unique opportunity for us, one that would allow us to "give back" without having to drive across town. Here's the deal: there is a candidate with Asperger's Syndrome who has very specific skills that we could use. Do we make her an offer? Before you weigh in with your input, I wanted to show you an interview with Dr. Temple Grandin. One-third of all meat companies in America use her equipment so that these animals can be more humanely treated. Dr. Grandin has Asperger's Syndrome. We also will look at a brief clip of Tom Cruise and Dustin Hoffman in the movie 'Rain Man.'

"We need to understand that if we do decide to hire Shirley, it will be because she is qualified. We wouldn't be doing charity; we would welcome a fellow human being with full rights. At the same time, we must realize that it may require us to modify our communication styles. Let's watch the interview and the movie clip."

> One hour later Chanél phoned HR, "This group is healthy enough to allow Shirley some compensation for her processing style. By the way, Frank, who uses a walker, quoted First Lady Roslyn Carter, who said, 'Mental conditions need to be put in the same status as physical handicaps.' That shifted the group. They can see Frank's physical condition; now they will learn to understand Shirley, who has an invisible handicap."

Travel Log

Leader's Traits and Self Care

A leader accepts the fact that stereotyping will naturally occur and she leads the group past surface prejudices and bias into seeing themselves as full, multi-faceted humans. Leadership is shared and liaisons are plentiful.

- The healthier the person-in-charge, the greater the chances that the group will also be healthy. She is committed to being a life-long learner.

- The healthy person-in-charge educates her unconscious mind by reviewing and reflecting on her day from an objective, dissociated viewpoint (3rd person). And she rehearses the future in an associated state (1st person) as she generates options for the next time a similar situation arises.

- She has trained herself to know when to trust her instincts and when not to.

- She is aware of her energy and seeks to take care of herself

A group's location on the Issue-People axis is very fluid. Over time, the group could operate in any of the quadrants: healthy, cat functional, dog functional, and dysfunctional. The leader monitors where the group is at on any given day; she works to avoid the seven factors that lead to temporary dysfunctionality and the nine factors that lead to chronic dysfunction. Her goal is to lead the group into the healthy quadrant, where there is a balance between High Productivity and High Morale.

Management—The Key to a Healthy Group

The leader uses these key leadership strategies:

- She recognizes group dynamic patterns and has a wide range of cat and dog behaviors to respond with.

- Management is done based on what is best for the group's health. Management is best done by avoiding eye-contact (two-point communication); instead the person-in-charge directs the individual to look at a visual directive (three-point communication).

- The leader uses only the amount of power needed to start to shift the individual to appropriate behavior. As soon as the individual begins to comply, she switches to influence.

- The managed individual's dignity remains intact.

Notes

Chapter Eight
Negotiating for a Healthy Group

"The essence of mastering systems thinking...lies in seeing patterns where others only see events and forces to react to." Peter Senge [45]

Road Map

A leader has to negotiate with the system if his group is to be at least functional, and hopefully healthy. A system and a group each create their own culture of self-preserving, self-perpetuating and self-correcting tendencies. This explains how a unit can have a retreat, arrive at some insights, and pledge to change their culture, yet when they return to the office, they revert back to their same previous habits.

In the movie *2001 Space Odyssey* the crew realizes it will have to abort the space station. The computer that runs the space ship realizes that the "humans" are willing to destroy themselves—but the computer is designed to preserve the status quo. So in order to survive, the computer begins to eliminate the crew one-at-a-time. This movie example illustrates why it is so hard to change a culture. A culture is like that computer in that the natural tendency

---

To be respectful of gender equality and yet provide the reader with a fluid reading style, in this chapter the person-in-charge is referred to by male pronouns and other individuals are referred to by female pronouns.

of a culture is to remain the same and resist charge. Because of *cultural homeostasis*, the leader's negotiating tools have to be very effective. Chapter Eight offers seven perceptual tools that the person-in-charge uses when negotiating with the system to improve the health of a group. These tools can also be used to improve the health of the entire system.

1. System Affects Group

Systems influence the groups within the system. That influence can be positive or negative, so it is important to recognize when to increase and when to decrease the system's influence on your group.

2. Invisible Triangles

It is essential that a leader understand that his boss has her own triangle made up of her own boss and peers. Even though the boss's triangle is invisible at the time, these *people-not-present* are a factor in any decisions that come out of the negotiation. The leader takes into account that decisions affect those not present.

3. The Decision-making Process

A leader uses different strategies for each of the four phases of the decision-making process. The phases are: Gathering, Evaluating, Deciding and Implementing.

4. Patterns of Domination

The leader profits from understanding how his own innate credibility or approachability patterns can be an asset or liability based on which phase of the decision-making process the negotiation is in. A pattern that works beautifully in one phase can be disastrous when used at a different phrase in the negotiation process.

5. Linguistic-Neuro

Of special interest is a technique to covertly gather information without the other party knowing consciously that such a process is occurring.

6. Calibrating

Humans are much more complex then a generalized label of credible cat and approachable dog. The leader pays attention to his boss' baseline behaviors and memorizes them. This allows him to detect minimal cues as the boss is changing from her baseline behavior to a posture that is either more credible (*position*) or more approachable (*person*). The more accurately he can calibrate the other party, the more appropriately he can negotiate.

7. Power, Information and Time Patterns

There are three variables that influence a negotiation: power, information and time. The interplay of these three factors greatly influences the success of a negotiation.

Perceptual Tools

1. System Affects Group

8-1

A group can only be fully understood when the system that houses the group is understood. In the following graphic, the small triangle (group level) represents offices, departments, divisions, or locations. The larger triangle (system level) could be a company, an industry, or a culture.*

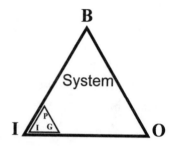

Everyone wants his environment to be at least functional. But each person defines his environment differently. The higher the organizational level in which the person operates, the more the person defines his environment as the entire system. This person is part of the system triangle, the BIO. A person at the middle levels of the organization rotates between being part of the BIO (system) and the PIG (group) triangles. And a person at the lower level of the organization sees himself as part of just the PIG level.

In all cases, you are negotiating either with a system or a group(s). Identifying the degree that the system and the group is functional or dysfunctional determines if you want more support or more latitude from the party you are negotiating with.

Since *Fast Track* focuses on groups, this section is written from the PIG perspective.

---

*I attempted to use "E" for Executive Level, or "C" for CEO or CFO… and settled on "B" because "BIO" is easier for people to remember (Boss, Individual units, Organization).

Three variables influence how the system affects a group:

• Group health: the group's functional vs. dysfunctional tendencies,

• System health: the system's functional vs. dysfunctional tendencies, and

• System influence: the system's high vs. low influence on the group.

An arrow pointing up means that the system has high influence on the group—which is great when the system is functional but bad when the system is dysfunctional. An arrow pointing down means that the system has low influence on the group—which is fine when the system is dysfunctional but not as helpful when the system is functional.

	Functional System		Dysfunctional System	
System's Level of Influence	**High** ↑	**Low** ↓	**Low** ↓	**High** ↑
Functional Group				
Dysfunctional Group				

The lower the number, the more likely it is that the group will be functional, as in variations 1, 2, 3, and 4. The higher the number, the more likely it is that the group will be dysfunctional, as in variations 5, 6, 7, and 8.

System's Level of Influence	Functional System		Dysfunctional System	
	High ↑	**Low** ↓	**Low** ↓	**High** ↑
Functional Group	1	2	3	5
Dysfunctional Group	4	6	7	8

A quick way to use the chart is to ask yourself:

A. Are you operating on the system level of an organization?

No. Go to Question B.

Yes. Ask, "Is the system functional?"

> No. If the system is not functional, decrease the influence of the system on individual groups so that variation three is more likely to occur. When the system becomes functional then increase the system's influence on groups.

> Yes. If the system is functional, increase the influence of the system on individual groups so that variations one and four are more likely.

B. Are you operating on the group level of an organization?

No. Go to Question A.

Yes. Ask, "Is the system functional?"

No. If the system is not functional, decrease the influence of the system. Isolate your group. Your target is variation six. Stay at a distance from the system's influence until the system is functional.

Yes. If the system is functional, increase the influence of the system on your group. Your target is variation one. Stay connected with the system's influence on your group.

If the system is functional, you next ask, "Is my group functional?"

Yes. If your group is functional, you are aiming for variation one or two.

No. If your group is not functional, you are aiming for variation four. Look for opportunities for the group to experience the functionality of the system.

Variations with Vignettes

As a person-in-charge look at the chart again and determine which of the eight variations represent your group. ONLY READ THAT VARIATION. Once you finish, continue on page 209 with an interview I did.

	Functional System		Dysfunctional System	
System's Level of Influence	High ↑	Low ↓	Low ↓	High ↑
Functional Group	1	2	3	5
Dysfunctional Group	4	6	7	8

8-2

Variation 1: Functional Group in a Functional System with High Influence

This is Camelot. Start moving the functional group towards being a healthy group.

The more a functional system has influence, the more likely it is that the group will remain functional.

In a functional system, if a group is functional, it is usually because the system is reinforcing the group's functional habits.

If a functional group, inside an influential functional system, starts operating in dysfunctional ways, it is likely that the dysfunctionality will be temporary because the system's positive influence will pull it back into functional ways.

If a functional group has tendencies towards becoming dysfunctional, yet the group does not become dysfunctional, usually it is because the positive system has high influence and doesn't allow the group to be dysfunctional.

Vignette: Functional Group in a Functional System with High Influence

Abe has been the satellite office manager for four years. Every quarter he fills out a written quality control report on the office activities for the previous three months. If there is a drop in performance, then in addition to the written quarterly report, a bi-weekly phone call with his regional manager is scheduled. During their phone call, Fran and Abe go over the possible reasons for the drop. If the drop is a surprise to both Abe and Fran, they switch to a monthly reporting system.

Abe welcomes the process because he understands that Fran is there to assist him—without blame or shame.

Variation 2: Functional Group in a Functional System with Low Influence

8-3

When the functional system has low influence, whenever a functional group dips into dysfunctional behaviors, it will take longer for the group to become functional again.

Encourage the system to have more contact and influence. This will move the group towards variation one.

Vignette: Functional Group in a Functional System with Low Influence

Ben was the first to open a branch office west of the Rocky Mountains. While he has turned a profit from the first anniversary on, he resents the fact that he didn't have any help from the home office to set up procedures. On his own, he has created a highly functioning office. Ben makes sure that employees are appreciated and have regular feedback on how their efforts satisfy the customers and positively affect the bottom line.

Ben has been ambivalent about increasing the monitoring from the home office. On the one hand, he is probably doing things *differently* than what the home office does. He hasn't wanted them to actually change his style. On the other hand, if something were to go wrong (for example, Ben having an extended illness), it would be helpful to have the home office more involved.

> Now Ben has decided to increase the involvement of the home office. He arranges to have the VP fly out once a year. He also arranged for the company's national conference to be held in his city. This increased the home office's awareness and interest in Ben's operations.

8-4

Variation 3: Functional Group in a Dysfunctional System with Low Influence

The functional group inside a dysfunctional system is more likely to remain functional if the group is isolated from the system's influence.

Do not increase contact with the system unless the system becomes functional. Note: When the system does become functional, if the system's influence is low then your group is variation two; if the newly-functional system has high influence then your group is variation one.

Vignette: Functional Group in a Dysfunctional System with Low Influence

Opening a new territory was a godsend for Cameron in that now he was much farther away from the dysfunctional home office. He had been given this opportunity because of his last district office success. While there, he had been reprimanded annually for having late reports and for ignoring the home office's cryptic requests. Ignoring the guidelines in the company manual is exactly what had made him successful, and he knew he was too successful to be fired.

Now with an office in a new territory, he has had valid excuses for not following the guidelines.

> Twice a year, he sends emails saying, "Still trying to understand the culture here. Will offer an alternative accounting system once I get settled in."
>
> He knows they cannot argue with him when he puts more money into the company's coffers than any other office.

Variation 4: Dysfunctional Group in a Functional System with High Influence

8-5

When a dysfunctional group climbs into functional behavior (variation one), it is likely to remain functional *if* it is part of a functional system that has high influence.

> ### Vignette: Dysfunctional Group in a Functional System with High Influence
>
> Dennis was a successful troubleshooter. When he inherited the motley crew at his current plant, he was challenged. Knowing that his propane company's commitment was to assist in any way possible, he waited for an opportunity for success. Fortuitously, the competitor in the same town decided to close their office. Dennis struck immediately. He brought in a cadre of the top salespeople. He matched each enthusiastic import with one of his laid-back-it-is-just-a-job employees.
>
> After two weeks of canvassing businesses and residents soliciting business, the imports' rubbing elbows with Dennis' staff worked. His employees caught the bug of enthusiasm and commitment.

It can be argued that variations three and four are equally difficult. Being in charge of a functional group in a dysfunctional system with low influence (variation three) is challenging. Being in charge of a dysfunctional group in a functional system with high influence (variation four) can be equally challenging.

8-6

Variation 5: Functional Group in a Dysfunctional System with High Influence

The more a functional group, inside an influential dysfunctional system, dips into operating dysfunctionally, the more likely it is that the group will stay there.

Decrease the contact and influence with the system. Move the group towards variation three.

Vignette: Functional Group in a Dysfunctional System with High Influence

Although Elson and Dennis worked for different companies, their high school friendship bypassed competitive boundaries. They often talked on the phone. When Dennis phoned to share his recent success with Elson, there was a knowing silence, then they simultaneously broke into laughter. They both knew that Dennis' strategy wouldn't have worked for Elson's situation.

Elson had a fine branch office except when the home office tried to interfere with what he was doing—which, unfortunately, was constant. The meddling was inane—busywork forms were required to be completed by Elson and his line chiefs. There was no relevance to the day-to-day operation of the plant. The paperwork dragon had to be slain.

Finally, at the risk of being insubordinate, Elson decided to fight "details with details." He started asking for greater clarification from the home office on the trivial aspects of each form. This tied up the home office's left-brain approach.

Elson also started making duplicate copies of weekly reports and just changing the dates. This minutia strategy freed Elson and his chiefs to concentrate more on the functioning of the group.

Variation 6: Dysfunctional Group in a Functional System with Low Influence

8-7

A dysfunctional group in a functional system with low influence on the group will tend to be isolated from the positive effects of the system and will therefore remain dysfunctional.

Increase the system's contact and influence to increase the likelihood that the group will move towards variation four.

Vignette: Dysfunctional Group in a Functional System with Low Influence

Frank almost quit the company last year. He had two bullies in his department—the classic rotten apples that affected the whole barrel. The company was dysfunctional and wouldn't support his firing of the two emotional thugs.

Frank didn't quit because he had heard that the corporation that bought out his company was very functional and actively supported middle managers. He wasn't disappointed when he met Samantha, his new straight-shooting. supervisor. But Frank's area was not the only one that Samantha had to clean up. She didn't have the time Frank needed for her to get a clear view of Frank's two problem employees.

Frank finally wrote her an email stating the current level and quality of productivity and what Frank's estimation of productivity could be with the two bullies removed. That caught her attention. She made Frank a deal, "Without you cuing me, if I can spot the two trouble makers myself then I will support you 100%."

The next day Samantha spent time around Frank's department. She easily detected the two members who were emotionally lazy and bullied people to do their work for them.

With Samantha's blessing, Frank delivered the bullies' walking papers the next day. Within a quarter, Frank's projections were realized.

It can be argued that variations five and six are equally difficult. Being in charge of a functional group in a dysfunctional system with high influence (variation five) is challenging. Being in charge of a dysfunctional group in a functional system that has low influence (variation six) can be equally challenging.

8-8

Variation 7: Dysfunctional Group in a Dysfunctional System with Low Influence

A group that is dysfunctional in a dysfunctional system with low influence could become functional if the person-in-charge has enough leadership. Move towards variation three.

Vignette: Dysfunctional Group in a Dysfunctional System with Low Influence

Gerry had prudently observed both good and bad supervisors in his 30 years at various warehouses of the same company. He had convinced himself that he could do a good job if given a chance. When his supervisor walked off the job in disgust one day, Gerry skipped lunch and immediately marched into the headquarters to see Pete. "You have a lousy crew at the East side warehouse. I know that you don't have the luxury to properly train a new supervisor and none of the current supervisors at the other warehouses want to be reassigned to that warehouse.. Let me stick my neck out and take over the position at my current pay scale until I can prove that I have what it takes to lead."

More than a little, stunned, Pete, the head honcho, silently sized up Gerry. Finally Pete said, "I will give you three months."

Gerry had anticipated that headquarters would not offer a realistic time line. He shot back with, "Nine months." And he calmly paused.

Pete, moved by Gerry's gutsy proposal, slowly uttered "OK."

Gerry, turned to leave and then, in a "Columbo-like" manner, he turned around at the door and said, "Hey, do us both a favor—stay away for at least six months." Without another word or glance, Gerry left.

8-9

Variation 8: Dysfunctional Group in a Dysfunctional System with High Influence

If a group that is capable of being functional is instead dysfunctional, usually it is because the dysfunctional system doesn't allow/reward the group for being functional.

If a group is dysfunctional, usually the system is dysfunctional and is reinforcing the group's dysfunctional habits.

If a dysfunctional group, inside an influential dysfunctional system, starts operating in functional ways, it is likely that the functionality will be temporary because of the system's negative influence.

The less influence a dysfunctional system has (variation seven), the more likely it is that a skilled person-in-charge will be able to convert a dysfunctional group into a functional group (variation six).

Vignette: Dysfunctional Group in a Dysfunctional System with High Influence

When Harry took the position of managing an ineffective sales force, he pledged to try it for a year. At the job interview, he had negotiated for certain support but during the first six months, what he was promised either was not forthcoming or came with too many strings attached.

Harry had tried several maneuvers to decrease the regional supervisors' visits to his office. The supervisors were relatives of the founders and didn't know how to be useful except to visit sites and take up managers' time. Harry especially resented it when he was expected to drop everything to go to lunch with these sycophants.

At the end of the 11th month, he turned in his resignation. Harry was proud of his effort and even prouder of how clear he was that it wasn't he that was dysfunctional—it was the system. He himself was quite healthy.

The following vignette illustrates how one person used the System Affects Group Chart.

Vignette: Loralie's Philosophy

Loralie is a veteran of both systems and groups. She allowed me to interview her for *Fast Track*. Michael: "Loralie, you are effective. Using the language of the System Affects Group model, will you explain how you are effective?"

"Michael, your chart actually allows me to articulate my intuitive reaction to Paul Malik. When Malik became the university's president three years ago, the Vocational Department was in bad shape although the university itself was in good shape. Now I understand why he was encouraged to increase his influence over the vocational department. Since he did that, the transitions of students into the work force have been smooth and effective.

"Yet at several high schools where the principals were dysfunctional, I advised the principals to decrease their influence over their Vocational Departments. This allowed me to be involved with the heads of those departments and directly influence those department heads.

> "Simply, if the system is functional, you encourage the system to increase its influence. On the other hand, if the system is dysfunctional, you decrease the system's influence on the group or department."

Travel Tips—System is Relative

Our level in the organization influences how we view "system" and "group." Those of us who operate on the upper organizational levels are most interested in making the whole system healthy. If we are a person-in-charge and times are difficult, then our boss represents the system. When frustrated, we vent towards her. If times are good, then the system is something off in the distance—it isn't necessarily our boss. Most people are more interested in the health of their immediate group members.[46]

2. Invisible Triangles

8-10

When the person-in-charge is talking to his immediate boss, on the surface it seems as if it is a one-on-one communication—just two people talking. But from an organizational viewpoint, the boss is not just a *person* she is also a *position.*[47] A leader knows he is the "individual" corner of his boss's invisible triangle. The boss might be thinking about the interaction from her hierarchical position, "What are the ramifications of this decision for the rest of my business unit?" A leader also realizes that his boss is the individual corner of the invisible triangle of *his* boss. (Just about everybody answers to somebody higher up.)

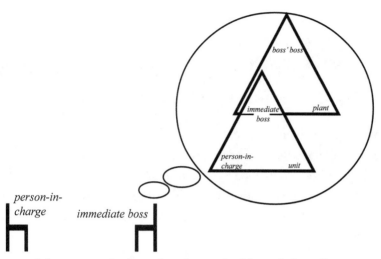

It becomes obvious that the typical boss is juggling many
invisible triangles at the same time. One way a leader can
become an astute negotiator is to realize that even when
communicating one-on-one, there are other triangles involved. They may be invisible, but they are always present.

8-11

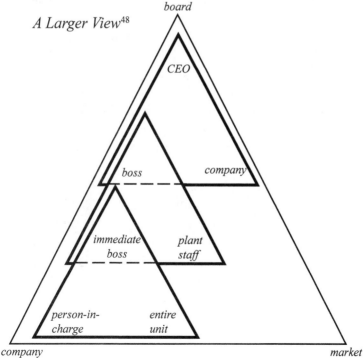

A Larger View[48]

The greatest blind spot that needs to be overcome is for each party to understand how the view looks from the other party's triangle(s).[49]

8-12

3. The Decision-making Process

Voice patterns are associated with the position someone has in relation to another person. The higher the position compared to another party, the more likely it is that the higher position will have the option of using the credible voice and the more likely it is that the lower position will use the approachable voice.

Vignette: Swiss Air Traffic Controllers

I did an in-service for the Swiss air traffic controllers. When we covered the concepts of credible and approachable voice patterns, there was a slow rolling chuckle that eventually surfaced. They were quietly laughing because the controllers had unearthed a subtle bias they didn't know they had.

The more the airline is from the Mediterranean culture, the more the pilots tend to have a rhythmic, approachable voice pattern. The more the airline is from northern Europe, the more the pilots speak with a flat, credible voice pattern.

They were laughing because the controller will often have the Mediterranean pilots confirm a second time that they have received the directive and are doing the maneuver. This is because of the controllers' instinctive distrust of those pilots' casual-sounding voice patterns.

The Four Phases and Voice Patterns[50]

8-13

A leader understands the connection between the two voice patterns and the four phases of the decision-making process. If the credible voice dominates during the Gathering phase, that phase is quickly left and the Evaluating and especially the Deciding phases are entered. If the approachable voice dominates then the group tends to procrastinate too long in the Gathering phase. In healthy groups where there are both approachable (⌒⌒⤴) and credible (⎯⎯⤵) voices actively present, the approachable voice people are highly valued during the Gathering phase and the credible voice people are highly valued during the Evaluating and especially the Deciding phases.[51]

8-14

4. Patterns of Domination

8-15

As previously mentioned, there are two voice patterns: credible and approachable. In public groups, the members of the group that have the most credible voices tend to dominate. One way to understand how the credible voice pattern dominates is to look at the decision-making process.

The approachable person is highly valued during the Gathering phase, but left out during the Deciding phase. Approachable people can increase their influence by learning to recognize when the decision-making process is nearing the end of the Gathering phase; they gradually switch to the non-verbal behaviors of the credible voice pattern such as sitting up straight, nodding less, and listening in silence. Likewise, it is smart for the credible people to increase their approachable behaviors during the Gathering phase so that they can elicit more information. Approachable behaviors include leaning forward, nodding the head, and making encouraging sounds when listening.

For the person-in-charge to be an effective leader, he must have the whole range of behaviors from *approachable* to *credible* and, even more importantly, he needs to remember when to use which pattern based on the phase of the decision-making process.

8-16

5. Linguistic-Neuro—Seeking Hidden Information

The Gathering phase of the Decision-making Process is often the single most important phase because one's ability to make effective decisions is based on the quality of the information gathered. When negotiating, a leader sometimes doesn't have permission to openly seek information. A back-up strategy is called Linguistic-Neuro. Instead of asking questions, he says several statements, each with different possibilities. The second and subsequent sentences begin with "...or...." As the statements are said, he watches the boss' reaction. The strategy is called "Linguistic" because the leader is using language (words) and "Neuro" because he is observing the boss' "neurological" response. If the boss stiffens, then she is showing a negative reaction, and if she relaxes, she is showing a positive response. In essence, the boss doesn't have to say anything because her non-verbals are speaking.

Linguistic-Neuro can be employed for a number of reasons. Sometimes the boss is not supposed to share information that she is privy to and yet the person-in-charge needs to know in order to be an effective negotiator. If he directly asks and the boss says, "Sorry, I cannot share that with you!" a gap between the two parties is created. The person-in-charge who can read body language learns the information without violating these covenants. Once the person-in-charge has a sense of the information he is seeking, he may want to verify his impression.

Linguistic-Neuro adds new meaning to the expression, "Up the creek without an or." And because it is both subtle and respectful is one of the best ways to "manage upwards."[52]

6. Calibrating

8-17

Calibrating is the ability to detect when a boss is changing from her *person* (approachable voice pattern) to her *position* (credible voice pattern) or the reverse. The more accurately the person-in-charge can read his boss, the more appropriate he can be. Also the distinction between person and position will free him from feeling hurt when the boss doesn't acknowledge or operate from the *personal* relationship between herself and the person-in-charge. An effective negotiator is aware of the following dynamics:

- When the boss increases her approachability, she is inviting the negotiator to match her style.

- When the boss increases her approachable pattern and the negotiator doesn't appropriately match her invitation, the boss could be *personally* hurt.

- When the boss is credible and is requesting input from the negotiator, if the negotiator matches with a credible style, the boss gives more credence to what the negotiator says.

- However, when the boss is credible and is sending information that is not to be questioned, the boss expects the negotiator to be approachable and agree with the boss. When the negotiator doesn't comply, the boss perceives that her position is not being honored.

Travel Tips—2 vs. 3-Point Communication

While the above is what the boss expects, *Fast Track* recommends that when we are looking at the boss (2-point), use approachable voice, and when we are looking at the piece of paper (3-point) which has a visual description of the difficult part of the negotiation, we can allow our voice to become more credible.

7. Power, Information and Time Patterns[53]

There are three variables that influence any negotiation: the Power of each party's position, the Information that each party has, and Time pressures. To say that the higher position has more ability to influence the decision than does the lower position is both accurate and simplistic. It is accurate in that the higher position has the *power* to make a decision. But a smart boss knows better than to arbitrarily wield power during a negotiation. She realizes that there are two other factors of equal and interacting importance: *information* and *time*. Both a boss and a person-in-charge need to be proactive in watching for these Power, Information and Time patterns; by recognizing them early, they will have more options as negotiators.

8-18

7A. Tension (Power) Easily Flows Downhill

A boss may send a message that in her mind is merely a *request*, not an ultimatum. But because of the organizational slope, the request, like a snowball, picks up tension or weight the farther it goes downhill. Middle management might inadvertently change the request into a directive.

In a healthy organization, all three parties (boss, middle management and the individual who fulfills the item) benefit from the practice of assigning a variety of weights (i.e. *request* vs. *directive* vs. *ultimatum*) to an item. This healthy approach prevents unnecessary havoc from occurring in the system/ group, such as stoppage of more critical projects. That way, when an item is tagged ultimatum, it will indeed get special treatment. This is because the different levels of the organization will be able to trust each other. In this atmosphere of trust, whenever people at lower levels foresee possible difficulties with an ultimatum, they are more likely to immediately convey their concerns to the boss. Then all levels can work towards a common solution.

7B. Information Needs Help to Go Uphill

8-19

The higher the rung the boss occupies, the more she lacks accurate *information* about what is really occurring. *Information* is like water: it cannot go uphill without assistance. A middle manager that can carry *information* to an uninformed boss and not shock the boss too much is highly valued.

7C. Lack of Time = Reverting to Power

8-20

When the boss runs out of *time*, she will revert to *power* even if she doesn't have enough *information*.

8-21

Vignette: Meeting

Carl has a deadline on making a decision. When he called the meeting for gathering input from those who will be affected by the decision, he knew it would be wise to write the time limitation on the white board. By having time constraints posted where all could see them, he figured that people would be more likely to stay within the time available.

The meeting starts on time. Within twenty minutes, Carl points and looks at the board while saying, "Based on the time we have left, what else do we want to explore?" By referencing the written *time* information, the board is like the bad guy. And by doing it before the actual ending time, he is utilizing the fairness ingredient of "letting people know what is coming before it actually gets here."

8-22

7D. Pressure = Withholding Information

Usually the person-in-charge don't like his boss to be too unilateral. However, this is what a boss tends to do when pressed for time. The tension can be either because the boss has a lot on her seasonal plate or because the specific meeting has taken too long. The boss non-verbally signals that she is switching to her authority role by increasing her credible attributes. Statistically, when the negotiator is surprised by the boss abruptly switching to power, his urge is to withhold information.

7E. Levels of Responsibilities

The Lower Rungs Switch to "Person" Sooner

8-23

This section adds the concept of Power, Information and Time to Seasonal Dysfunction (page 88).

Different levels of an organization (power) sustain their energy over the time of the project, protocol, or product. Often the finalizing of a project, protocol, or product will leave everyone exhausted. Salaried personnel often use athletic and military terms to describe the process: "a struggle," "a battle," or "a campaign." As the final stages are approached, the lower an individual's level of responsibility, the sooner he will switch from his position of responsibility back to his person.

> *Levels of Responsibility*
>
> Upper Manager—Highest
>
> Middle Manager
>
> Lower Rungs—Lowest

All organizational levels need to be aware that when the levels of responsibility are seasonally different (*time*), there tends to be less empathy between the levels. For instance, two days before finishing a long and exhausting project/protocol/product, there is a growing schism between the middle managers and their subordinates. But the middle managers and bosses are still aligned. If the boss calls an emergency meeting with two days to go, and the boss sends out power management directives such as, "Let's make ourselves visible—we need to better monitor the quality of the work," or "Let's build in accountability for their productivity," the middle managers will agree with the boss.

However, during the last hours of finishing, some of the middle managers have already switched to being right-brain oriented. They are thinking about their own private world; they are planning how they are going to reward themselves for their self-sacrificing. These middle managers are now identifying more with the lower rung employees than with the upper management. If the upper management calls an emergency meeting now, instead of at "two days to go," many middle managers will perceive the top boss as "uptight" and "unreal."

> *"Timing" isn't everything, but it is one of three variables of negotiation.*

8-24

Subordinate's Expectations

Subordinate's Expectations is a corollary to the previous pattern. The person-in-charge on the lower-rung needs to understand that when there are breaks in the routines, he becomes more *person* while at the same time his boss becomes more *position*. The gap can widen enough so that the person-in-charge may do well to stay away from the boss because right now, she doesn't have *time*. The person-in-charge realistically cannot expect the boss to exhibit much sensitivity during these times, so he wisely decides to "lay low." If he is around the boss, he shouldn't expect a lot of *personal warmth* (sympathy, understanding, humor) from her. During the boss' busy time, it is difficult to access the relationship level of the communication with the boss. Person-to-person communication is more likely to occur—if at all—after the person-in-charge acknowledges how full the boss' plate is. It is nearly impossible to establish a new relationship during the hectic time slots.

The boss views herself as having responsibilities, whereas the subordinates see the higher position as having actual *power.* A smart negotiator sees that the other position has a different yet perfectly reasonable perception. One of *Fast Track's* key insights is that reducing surprise is beneficial. This is apart from whether the negotiator can do anything about what occurring. By not being surprised, the negotiator continues to breathe well. Getting oxygen to the brain allows the negotiator to be flexible. This insight is summarized with *Fast Track's* axiom that there can be "Insights without Solutions." My best *professional* days are the ones in which I didn't get my outcomes. I was *professional* in that I didn't take the lack of results *personally.*

Utilization of Relationship

8-25

Since the relationship is the highest level of communication, either person can remind the other of their past and/ or future relationship. Successfully accessing the relationship level increases the latitude of solutions and the options of how to proceed.

Referring to an established relationship:

"Frank, we have worked with each other for three years. I know we are going through a rough spell right now. I would ask us to get through our pending deadline. Then give ourselves some time to recover. After that, we can talk about how we might handle similar situations better in the future."

Referring to a future relationship:

"Janet, at the start of this long project, may I say how much I am looking forward to working with you. While there will inevitably be ups and downs, I am confident we will learn to adjust to each other's style. I look forward to an on-going relationship with you."

Of course, it benefits both parties to have the relationship established before the crisis arises.

"Hank, thank you for phoning about the reimbursable invoice. I agree that the flight, car rental, and lodging seem high. Thanks for knowing that we can be honest with each other. Let me double check the receipts and I will get back to you."

If the establishment of the relationship had certain non-verbals associated with it, it is useful to access those when reaccessing the relationship level. In the following example, the restaurant is the non-verbal.

"Sally, I remember when we sat at Salty's Restaurant four years ago and toasted the start of our consultancy. And we have had great success until this contract where we have under bid. We both want to continue with our relationship. And at the same time, let's sort out how each of us will need to absorb this loss. After the next contract, may I treat us to another meal at Salty's?"

8-26

Superior Having Meetings

The superior should have meetings with subordinates before a break in the routine starts to occur. This is because the superior's and subordinates' *needs and motivations* are more aligned beforehand than they are after the break in routines.

Travel Log

A manager who doesn't attempt to negotiate with superiors because "they have all the power," is simply naive. He is displaying the self-created limitations of a culture that tends not to engage in the politics of decision-making.[54] Chapter Eight helps the person-in-charge avoid feeling like a "victim" of those in power. Negotiators can empower themselves with this chapter's mental constructs.

1. System Affects Group

When a group is part of a functional system, the leader negotiates for needed support. He welcomes opportunities for the system to influence his group. But when a group is part of a dysfunctional system, the leader negotiates for needed latitude. He decreases the system's influence on his group so he can have a better chance of getting the group to be functional.

2. Invisible Triangles

An effective negotiator is aware that each party is operating from different perspectives and considerations. The perspectives and considerations are graphically represented by a triangle.

- Negotiation involves invisible triangles. The negotiator is aware of his own triangle as well as his boss' triangle and the combination of both triangles.

- When the communication isn't productive, it is often because each party is only thinking of his or her own triangle.

- The lower-rung individual has a tendency to think that conversations with bosses are egalitarian, whereas the high-rung individual views discussions as having a hierarchical structure.

- One of our goals is to avoid surprises by being able to predict what is likely to happen. By being aware of the boss' triangle, the negotiator can be better aware of his boss' pressures and, as a result, the boss might respond more favorably to his requests.

3. The Decision-making Process

There are four phases of the decision-making process. The negotiator addresses each phase by using the appropriate credible or approachable style.

Gathering—use an approachable (dog) style

Evaluating and Deciding—use a credible (cat) style

Implementing (seeking feedback)—use an approachable (dog) style

4. Voice Patterns of Domination

The person with the more credible style tends to dominate the person with the more approachable style. A leader recognizes the value of being able to operate from both styles depending on the situation. A leader uses the credible style when sending information, and the approachable style when seeking information.

5. Linguistic-Neuro

When a leader needs information and the other person is withholding, he switches from questions to statements that represent several possibilities. The leader pauses after each possibility and notices the listener's breathing. If the individual breathes high and shallow, emphasizes an inhalation, or holds his breath, the item is associated with negative importance. During the pause, if the individual breathes deep, from low in the abdomen, emphasizes an exhalation, or breathes fluidly, the item is associated with positive importance.

6. Calibrating

Calibrating is a skill that allows the leader to *read* each individual he interacts with. The leader memorizes the other person's baseline behaviors. Any increase in the credible behaviors indicates the person is moving towards her *position.* Any increase in the approachable behaviors indicates the person is moving towards her *person.* The leader takes these cues and responds appropriately.

Fast Track suggests that the negotiator put controversial topics on paper. When he looks at the paper he is credible. When he looks at the boss he is approachable.

7. Power, Information and Time Patterns

Power, information, and time are the three variables that influence any negotiation. Five patterns that occur within the Power-Information-Time system were listed. An effective negotiator must be aware of how these patterns influences the group's health

The hardest lesson to learn is that we don't get to determine how functional or healthy our group will be. The good news is that as a person-in-charge, we can be functional/healthy even if our group isn't. In fact, the more we are functional/healthy, the more likely the group/system can be functional/healthy.

Epilogue: Making Sense

As a youngster sitting in a movie theater, I remember being mesmerized when Danny Kaye ended the movie singing, "Five Little Pennies." As I end this book, I leave you with my version of the wisdom of five cents/senses.

A Sense of Practicality

Fast Track is not intended to be an academic treatise. This work is my distilment of observing group behaviors on four continents over 40 years. My work is in the vein of zoologist Desmond Morris, whose popular book of yesteryear, *The Naked Ape,* was not intended to be a "scientific" work. Rather, it was his commentary on the human condition. How scientific is *Fast Track*? That depends on how you define "scientific." There is research done at universities and then there is applied research. At best, I am an applied researcher. I am encouraged by the quote,

> *In theory,*
> *there is no difference between theory and practice.*
> *In practice, there is.*[55]

A Sense of Sensibility

Malcolm Gladwell opens his book, *Blink*, with three postulates:

- Our first impression, intuition, gut reaction, unconscious mind is powerful.

- While our unconscious mind greatly influences, it is fallible.

- We have to educate our intuition for it to be accurate.

Fast Track educates our perception so that what we sense about group dynamics is accurate. When we are unfamiliar with the culture, our lack of familiarity causes our instincts to be unreliable. Our instincts are equally skewed when our surroundings are too familiar. As Margaret Mead said, "If a fish were an anthropologist, the last thing it would ever discover is water."

To educate our instincts about both the unfamiliar and familiar we first need to understand our two separate but over-lapping intelligences: **inter**-personal and **intra**-personal. Inter-personal intelligence is our ability to notice group dynamics; it is an external focus. Intra-personal intelligence is our contact with ourselves; it is an internal focus. It is what creative people tap into. Gary Larson of the "Far Side" cartoon strip was asked where he got his ideas. He responded, "I don't know but they better keep coming, I have deadlines."[56]

Whether we are in an unfamiliar environment or one so familiar we can't see the forest for the trees, we live life based on how we feel. We have to resist letting our feelings filter our perception. When our feelings (intra-personal intelligence) lead our perception (inter-personal intelligence) we have a faulty sequence, one that can be woefully dangerous and foolish.

At the same time being a robot, devoid of feelings, is equally foolish. We need to balance our head and heart. We have to be sensible about our perception.

> *Information without interpretation is useless.*
> *Interpretation without evidence is dangerous.*

A Sense of Predictability

My work is based on non-verbal intelligence, which is the ability to recognize, label, predict, and respond to patterns of communication. The cat in us is drawn to the *response* level. Instead, I would strongly recommend that we focus on the *predict* level as it enables us to reduces surprises. When we are surprised we breathe high, thus releasing flight or fight chemicals. Our flexibility is decreased. Surprise is the enemy of competence. Being able to predict is the antidote for surprise.

Sometimes our knowledge only allows us to predict what is about to happen even if it is an outcome we don't want. But by not being surprised we continue to breathe well and are be more successful in the long run. Success is often the by-product of focusing on effort—John Wooden, the winningest collegiate basketball coach of all time, never mentioned "winning."

A Sense of Ethics

I am a great fan of Nelson Mandela. Mandela is associated with the quote,[57]

> *Our deepest fear is not that we are inadequate.*
> *Our deepest fear is that we are powerful*
> *beyond measure.*
> *It is our light, not our darkness,*
> *that most frightens us.*

> *We ask ourselves, "Who am I to be brilliant,*
> *gorgeous, talented and fabulous?"*
> *...And as we let our own light shine, we*
> *unconsciously give other people permission to do the*
> *same. As we are liberated from our own fear, our*
> *presence automatically liberates others.*

My hope is that *Fast Track's* knowledge (both perception and responses) will liberate us by shining a light on group dynamics. And as dynamics of a group become transparent, our leadership can be powerful beyond measure.

Walt Disney's Sorcerer's Apprentice was powerful. The sorcerer's apprentice had the knowledge to get brooms to carry in buckets of water. But knowledge without ethics can lead to narcissistic arrogance. The apprentice needed to control himself. He needed to have an ethical framework for why the brooms were bringing in the water and guidelines as to how much water was needed. *Fast Track* provides us with the knowledge to get groups to carry out tasks. My final wish is that

> *Our ethical standards will always increase*
> *ahead of our knowledge base.*

A Sense of Appreciation

Fast Track shares my educated intuition about managing groups. But all of us have drunk from wells that others have dug and been warmed by fires that others have built. *Fast Track* is my advancement of what others have exposed me to. Hopefully, *Fast Track* will be part of the long tradition of one model standing on the shoulders of a previous model and will serve as a basis for future insights. I humbly both welcome and encourage critical refinements and disagreements with my findings.

End Notes

1. (p. 21) See Michael Grinder, *ENVoY, Your Personal Guide to Classroom Management* (Battle Ground: MGA, 1993), 14.

2. (p. 21) Michael Grinder, *The Elusive Obvious* (Battle Ground: MGA, 2007), 67.

3. (p. 21) Ibid., 76.

4. (p. 23) Ibid., 166.

5. (p. 26) Michael Grinder, *Charisma—The Art of Relationships* (Battle Ground: MGA, 2004). Using the concept of cats and dogs, the unison with dog-oriented individuals will be more uniform than with cat-oriented individuals. As Dr. Bill Sommers says, "Dogs will behave with a pack, but it is an oxymoron to say one can 'herd cats.'"

6. (p. 33) More details are found in *Charisma—The Art of Relationships,* third edition, 6.

7. (p. 35) Flat voice that curls down at the end.

8. (p. 35) Rhythmic voice that curls up at the end.

p. (p. 35) There are many advantages to having a formed group. See *Pushing a Group*, p. 113. And see *Share Leadership*, p. 137.

10. (p. 37) Judith DeLozier originated the quote.

11. (p. 51) The terms "leader" and "barometer" are descriptions of different functions in a group. Later, a third role will be introduced—a liaison. An individual could be a leader, a barometer, a liaison, none of them, two of them, or all three.

12. (p. 52) In groups of more than 16 people,

there are 4-6 people the person-in-charge needs to monitor. These 4-6 are the leaders and barometers of the important subgroups. Each culture determines which subgroups are important.

13. (p. 53) These maneuvers are called *Decontamination* and *Break and Breathe*. See *The Elusive Obvious*, 76 and 150.

14. (p. 75) See *Fostered Leaders*, 53.

15. (p. 85) See *How Well are the Individual Members Known?* 22.

16. (p. 93) Each author has written several books; Tannen is famous for *You Just Don't Understand* and Gray for *Men are from Mars, Women from Venus.*

17. (p. 96) For more details on breathing, see *The Elusive Obvious*, 114-129.

18. (p. 103) For more details on breathing, see *The Elusive Obvious*, 114-129.

19. (p. 104) See page 164.

20. (p. 111) For more details, see *The Elusive Obvious*, 81.

21. (p. 114) Donald Walker, *Never Try To Teach a Pig to Sing...Wit and Wisdom for Leaders* (Holt, Michigan: Partners Publishers Group, 1998).

22. (p. 117) *The Elusive Obvious*, 114, 164.

23. (p. 122) Suzette Elgin, *Staying Well With The Gentle Art of Verbal Self-Defense* (New York: Prentice Hall, MJF Books, 1997), 166.

24. (p. 126) Herb Cohen, *You Can Negotiate Anything* (New York: Bantam Books, 1982).

25. (p. 127) The two hooks, marking eye contact and being verbal while managing, increase the likelihood of escalation.

26. (p. 128) For example, "You are a good worker" is praise while "You have four of the six orders finished" is encouragement.

27. (p. 129) *Imploding* is worse on the person-in-charge.

28. (p. 129) Colin Powell, with Joseph Persico, *My American Journey* (New York: Ballantine Books, 2003).

29. (p. 130) Steven B. Karpman, "Fairy tales and script drama analysis," in *Transactional Analysis Bulletin* (San Francisco: 1968), #7, 39-43.

30. (p. 131) See *Protecting an Individual*, 141.

31. (p. 140) Malcolm Gladwell, *Blink* (New York: Little, Brown and Company, 2005), 85-86.

32. (p. 142) *Charisma*, 53.

33. (p. 144) From a private conversation with a Civil War buff, June, 2008.

34. (p. 149) *Blink*, 14-15.

35. (p. 150) "When to go with your gut," *Prevention Magazine* (June 2008), 108.

36. (p. 157) Being *associated* is correlated with Howard Gardner's Intrapersonal Intelligence. Being *dissociated* allows the person-in-charge to increase his Interpersonal Intelligence (awareness of group dynamics).

37. (p. 158) Look at *Victim* on page 126. The seasons affect the person-in-charge as well as the people above and below her.

38. (p. 164) Three-point management preserves the relationship while increasing compliance on a behavioral level.

39. (p. 165) For a more detailed listing of non-verbals to use when communicating with BIG CATS, see *Charisma*, 151-160.

40. (p. 170) In Roman times, a child of wealth had a slave assigned to him as a muse-playmate. When the child was naughty, the parents would likely whip the slave. Because the child wouldn't want to see his "friend" hurt, he was likely to change.

41. (p. 180) For more details, see *The Elusive Obvious*, 81.

42. (p. 181) Reference to *Levels of Leadership*, 186.

43. (p. 182) Allen Shamblin and Steve Seskin, "Life's a Dance," from the album *Life's a Dance*. (Atlantic, 1992).

44. (p. 186) From John Grinder and Richard Bandler's study of Milton Erickson.

45. (p. 193) Peter Senge, et al, *The Fifth Discipline Field Book* (New York: Doubleday, 1994).

46. (p. 210) Most people inside an organization are more interested in the health of their immediate group than the overall health of the organization/system. To test this statement, ask people the following question: If you could select only one choice, which would you pick? (A) The people in your immediate work group being functional (or healthy); (B) The people immediately above you being functional (or healthy); (C) The organization being functional (or healthy). People select the first choice (A) 90% of the time.

47. (p. 210) See *Calibrating* p. 215

48. (p. 211) Contributed by Rachel Babbs, Michael Grinder & Associates trainer and coach.

49. (p. 212) Steven R. Covey, *Seven Habits of Highly Effective People* (New York: Simon & Schuster, 1989).

50. (p. 213) An easy way to remember the four phases is to convert the initial letters of each phase into the acronym GEDI (pronounced like "Jedi Warrior" in *Star Wars).*

51. (p. 213) In my opinion, we will never have a "learning community" (from Peter Senge) if the top echelon maintains the credible voice pattern. In his book, *The Creative Brain* (England: Atlantic Books, 1999) Ned Hermann advocates that CEOs be female because they have better access to both sides of the brain.

52. (p. 215) The corporate term for a lower position effectively influencing a superior.

53. (p. 216) The three variables of negotiation are taken from Herb Cohen's book, *You can Negotiate Anything.*

54. (p. 223) Contact information for Arielle Essex: Arielle@practicalmiracles.com.

55. (p. 227) Two sources: Jan L.A. van de Snepscheut (Cal Tech, head of computer science) and Yogi Berra.

56. (p. 228) Heard during a Q & A presentation, Portland, Oregon.

57. (p. 229) Taken from a program called "Course in Miracles."

Bibliography

Bateson, Gregory. (1972). *Steps to an Ecology of Mind*. The University of Chicago Press.

Bennis, Warren G. (1997). *Managing People is Like Herding Cats*. Provo, UT: Executive Excellence Publishing.

Cohen, Herb. (1982).*You Can Negotiate Anything* New York: Bantam Books.

Covey, Stephen R. (1989). *Seven Habits of Highly Effective People*. New York: Simon & Schuster.

Elgin, Suzette. (1997). *Staying Well With The Gentle Art of Verbal Self-Defense*. New York: Prentice Hall, MJF Books.

Fisher, Roger and Sharp, Alan. (1999). *Getting it Done*. New York: Harper Business.

Fisher, Roger and Ury, William. (1983). *Getting to Yes*. New York: Penguin Books.

Gardner, Howard. (1993). *Multiple Intelligences*. New York: Basic Books.

Gladwell, Malcolm. (2005) *Blink: The Power of Thinking Without Thinking*. New York: Little, Brown and Company.

Gottman, John. (2001). *The Relationship Cure*. New York: Crown Publishers.

Gray, John. (1992). *Men are From Mars, Woman are From Venus*. NY: Harper Collins.

Grinder, Michael. (2007). *The Elusive Obvious*. Battle Ground, WA: MGA Publishers.

_____(2007) *ENVoY*, eighth edition. Battle Ground, WA: MGA Publishers.

_____(2009) *Charisma—The Art of Relationships*, third edition. Battle Ground, WA: MGA Publishers.

Herrmann, Ned. (1991). *The Creative Brain*. Lake Lure: Brainbooks.

Hodgkinson, Gerard. (2008). "When to go with your gut," *Prevention Magazine*.

Karpman, Steven B. (1968) "Fairy Tales and Script Drama Analysis," in *Transactional Analysis Bulletin*. San Francisco.

Kouzes, James M. and Posner, Barry Z. (1993). *Credibility*. San Francisco: Jossey-Bass Publishers.

Lara, Adair. (1996). "When Children Turn Into Cats." *San Francisco Chronicle*.

Luft, Joseph. (1969). *Of Human Interaction*. New York: National Press Books.

Miller, George. (1956). "The Magical Number Seven, Plus or Minus Two" in *Psychological Review*, p. 63.

Miller, Julie and Essex, Arielle. (2008). *Make the Juice Worth the Squeeze*. MROI

Miller, Philip (2008) *The Really Good Fun Cartoon Book of NLP*. Wales: Crown House Publishing, Ltd.

Powell, Colin and Persico, Joseph. (2003). *My American Journey*. New York: Ballantine Books.

Rogers, Carl R. (1961) *On Becoming a Person: A Therapist's View of Psychotherapy*. Boston: Houghton Mifflin.

Schultz, Charles M. (1980) *Charlie Brown, Snoopy and Me*. New York: Doubleday & Company, Inc.

Senge, Peter. (1990). *The Fifth Discipline*. New York: Doubleday Current.

Shamblin, Allen and Steve Seskin. (1992). "Life's a Dance" from the album *Life's a Dance*. Atlantic.

Tannen, Deborah. (1990). *You Just Don't Understand*. New York: Ballantine Books, Inc.

Tuckman, Bruce. (1965). "Developmental Sequence in Small Groups" in *Psychological Bulletin*.

Walker, Donald. (1996). *Never Try to Teach a Pig to Sing*. San Diego, CA: Lathrop Press.

Wheatley, Margaret. (1992). *Leadership and the New Science*. San Francisco: Berrett-Koehler Publishers.

Zoller, K. & Landry, C. (2010). Choreography of Presenting: *7 Essential Abilities of Effective Presenters*. Thousand Oaks, CA: Corwin Press.

Index

Managing Groups—The Inside Track

The longer version of *Fast Track* is *Managing Groups—The Inside Track*. It is over 500 pages with twice the insights. It is the version used in Michael's certification program. Book.

The Elusive Obvious—The Science of Non Verbal Communication

Brimming with practical ideas you can try today, *The Elusive Obvious* reveals the twenty-one non-verbals that are found at the heart of all communication models, no matter how different they may appear on the surface.

Easy to read and understand, this ground-breaking book explores the roots and mastery of non-verbal behaviors that make up 90% of all communication. The non-verbals presented form the foundation of influence and success in communication.

Written as a blend of textbook and instruction manual, *The Elusive Obvious* is a resource for trainers, managers, students, teachers, and researchers in non-verbal communication.

The Elusive Obvious products include: Book, DVD, Laminates, Flash Cards and Album.

Charisma—The Art of Relationships

Success still comes down to relationships. Rich in practical, immediately applicable skills, *Charisma* uses your intuitive knowledge of pets to help you easily develop relationships with anyone you meet. Charisma products include: Book, DVD, Audio CDs and Album.

Classroom Management Trilogy

Michael visited 6,000 classrooms to find out what the most effective teachers have in common. He formulated what he observed into clear management strategies, then published the results in this trilogy:

- *A Cat In The Dog House*—How to establish relationships with the hard-to-reach students.

- *ENVoY*—How to preserve the relationships while managing. Book, DVD, Pamphlets, Inservice Kit.

- *A Healthy Classroom*—How to utilize relationships between the students—group dynamics.

Visit our website www.michaelgrinder.com

Free *Fast Track*, *The Elusive Obvious* and *Charisma* worksheets, downloadable screen savers, study guide for cadre groups, blogs and video footage. Schedule of Michael's classes. Latest announcements. Additional products.